I0430060

DEPARTMENT OF THE NAVY
OFFICE OF THE CHIEF OF NAVAL OPERATIONS
2000 NAVY PENTAGON
WASHINGTON, DC 20350-2000

AND

HEADQUARTERS UNITED STATES MARINE CORPS
3000 MARINE CORPS PENTAGON
WASHINGTON, DC 20350-3000

NAVY LASER HAZARDS CONTROL PROGRAM

DEPARTMENT OF THE NAVY
OFFICE OF THE CHIEF OF NAVAL OPERATIONS
2000 NAVY PENTAGON
WASHINGTON, DC 20350-2000

AND

HEADQUARTERS UNITED STATES MARINE CORPS
3000 MARINE CORPS PENTAGON
WASHINGTON, DC 20350-3000

OPNAVINST 5100.27B
MCO 5104.1C
CNO(N09F)/CMC(SD)
2 May 2008

OPNAV INSTRUCTION 5100.27B
MARINE CORPS ORDER 5104.1C

From: Chief of Naval Operations
        Commandant of the Marine Corps

Subj: NAVY LASER HAZARDS CONTROL PROGRAM

Ref: (a) 21 CFR 1040, Performance Standard for Light Emitting
            Products
        (b) ANSI Z136.1, Safe Use of Lasers (NOTAL)
        (c) SECNAVINST 5100.14D
        (d) 29 CFR 1926.54 and 1926.102(b,) Safety and Health
            Regulations for Construction
        (e) OPNAVINST 5100.23G, chapter 22
        (f) OPNAVINST 5100.19E, chapter B9
        (g) OPNAVINST 5102.1D/MCO P5102.1B, Navy and Marine Corps
            Mishap and Safety Investigation Reporting and Record
            Keeping Manual
        (h) MIL-STD-882D, Department of Defense Standard Practice
            for System Safety
        (i) OPNAVINST 3500.39B
        (j) MIL-HDBK-828A, Department of Defense Handbook Laser
            Safety on Ranges and in Other Outdoor Areas
        (k) DoD 4160.21-M, Defense Materiel Disposition Manual,
            of August 1997
        (l) DoD 4160.21-M-1, Defense Demilitarization Manual, of
            October 1991
        (m) BUMEDINST 6470.23, Medical Management of Non-Ionizing
            Radiation Casualties
        (n) ANSI Z136.3, Safe Use of Lasers in Health Care
            Facilities (NOTAL)
        (o) BUMEDINST 6470.19A, Laser Safety at Military
            Facilities and Research Laboratories
        (p) ANSI Z136.2, Safe Use of Optical Fiber Communication
            Systems Utilizing Laser Diode and LED Sources (NOTAL)
        (q) SECNAV M-5210.1, Department of the Navy Records
            Management Program

DISTRIBUTION STATEMENT A: Approved for public release; distribution
is unlimited.

(r) SECNAV M-5210.2, Department of the Navy Standard
    Subject Identification Code (SSIC) Manual
(s) NAVMC DIR 5210.11E, Marine Corps Records Management
    Program Manual

Encl: (1) Laser System Safety Officer Training Requirements
      (2) Laser Safety Design Requirement Checklists
      (3) Requirements and Procedures of the Laser Safety
          Review Board (LSRB)
      (4) Guidelines for Submission of a Laser Data Package and
          Presentation at the LSRB Meeting
      (5) Military Laser Exemption Notification Format
      (6) Activity Laser Hazard Control Program
      (7) General Requirements for Laser Hazard Control
      (8) Safety Requirements for Military Laser Ranges
      (9) Laboratory Laser Use and Laser Maintenance
          Requirements
      (10) Example of Military Exempt Laser Inventory Format
      (11) Example of Non-Military Exempt Class 3B and Class 4
           Laser Inventory Format
      (12) Laser Safety Requirements Summary

1. Purpose. To prescribe Navy and Marine Corps policy and
guidance in the identification and control of laser radiation
hazards. This instruction has been administratively revised and
should be read in its entirety.

2. Cancellation. OPNAVINST 5100.27A/MCO 5104.1B.

3. Background. The widespread use of lasers in both commercial
and military applications has increased the probability of
injury from exposure to laser radiation. References (a) through
(p) provide controls over laser design and operation for
protection of personnel and equipment or contain specific
information on various laser safety subjects. Enclosures (1)
through (12) provide requirements and guidance on various
aspects of the Navy Laser Hazards Control Program.

4. Scope. The provisions of this directive are mandatory for
all Navy and Marine Corps activities. They apply to the design,
use, and disposal of all equipment and systems capable of
producing laser radiation, including laser fiber optics and
system support equipment. Directed energy weapons that emit

2

laser radiation and other high-energy laser systems are subject to the requirements of this directive. Medical, industrial, and construction laser systems that have no military-specific applications are exempted from this instruction. This document has been coordinated with all members of the Navy Laser Safety Review Board (LSRB).

5. Definitions

   a. Administrative Laser Safety Officer (ALSO). One who has successfully completed an Administrative Lead Agent (ALA) and Lead Navy Technical Laboratory (LNTL)-approved ALSO course. See enclosure (1).

   b. Laser. An acronym for light amplification by stimulated emission of radiation. Any device that can be made to produce or amplify electromagnetic radiation in the X-ray, ultraviolet, visible, and infrared or other portions of the spectrum by the process of stimulated emission of photons.

   c. Laser Classifications. There are four laser hazard classifications that determine the required extent of radiation safety controls. These range from class 1 lasers that are safe for direct beam viewing under most conditions to class 4 lasers that require the strictest of controls. Laser product classification pertains to intended use only. When a laser product is disassembled for maintenance, etc., and protective features removed, the laser classification may change to a more hazardous class. Details concerning laser classification are contained in references (a) and (b). Controls for each class are addressed in this instruction and in references (b) through (f).

   d. Laser Safety Specialist (LSS). One who has successfully completed the ALA and LNTL-approved LSS course. The Technical Laser Safety Officer (TLSO) course is a prerequisite for the LSS course. The LSS qualification is an advanced laser system safety officer. An LSS possesses the technical knowledge required to perform laser measurements, hazard evaluations, and calculations. See enclosure (1).

   e. Laser System Safety Officer (LSSO). A generic term used throughout this instruction. It can refer to personnel functioning as an ALSO, TLSO, LSS or Range Laser Safety Specialist (RLSS).

    f. <u>Military Exempt Lasers</u>. Lasers designed for actual combat, combat training operations, or classified in the interest of national security and are exempted from the requirements of reference (a). Military exempt laser systems must comply with the design requirements provided in enclosure (2).

    g. <u>Nominal Hazard Zone (NHZ)</u>. The volume of space within which the level of the direct, reflected, or scattered laser radiation may exceed the applicable Maximum Permissible Exposure (MPE) level.

    h. <u>Range Laser Safety Officer (RLSO)</u>. One who has successfully completed an ALA- and LNTL-approved TLSO course. An RLSO is a TLSO with assigned laser range management responsibilities as outlined in paragraph 5 of enclosure (8). RLSOs are qualified to perform the duties of an ALSO with emphasis on outdoor use of lasers. RLSOs are not qualified to perform laser or laser range hazard evaluations and calculations. See enclosure (1).

    i. <u>Range Laser Safety Specialist (RLSS)</u>. One who has successfully completed the ALA- and LNTL-approved RLSS course. The TLSO course is a prerequisite for the RLSS course. The RLSS possesses the technical knowledge required to perform laser range hazard evaluations and calculations required for laser range certification. See enclosure (1).

    j. <u>Technical Laser System Safety Officer (TLSO)</u>. One who has successfully completed an ALA- and LNTL-approved TLSO course. TLSOs are qualified to perform the duties of both ALSOs and RLSOs, but are not qualified to perform laser or laser range hazard evaluations and calculations. See enclosure (1).

    k. All other terms relating to lasers shall be those given in references (a) and (b).

6. <u>Policy</u>. Department of the Navy (DON) policy is to identify and control laser radiation hazards early during design and development as a matter of military necessity. DON policy is

also to ensure that personnel are not exposed to laser radiation in excess of the applicable MPE throughout the life cycle of laser systems, including research, design, testing, development, evaluation, acquisition, deployment, operation, support, maintenance, demilitarization and disposal.

7. Responsibilities

a. Administrative Lead Agent (ALA). The Bureau of Medicine and Surgery (BUMED)(Code M3B4) is the ALA within the DON. The ALA shall:

(1) Act as the primary point of contact and authority within the DON on non-technical laser safety issues.

(2) Represent the DON in tri-service and other inter-agency laser safety matters including laser radiation medical surveillance.

(3) Establish laser safety policy and guidance for the DON; and maintain membership on national and international standards setting boards and committees to ensure currency of Navy policy.

(4) Perform the duties of secretariat for the Navy LSRB as described in enclosure (3).

(5) Coordinate with the LSRB chair to schedule requested Board reviews to evaluate the safety parameters of laser systems during the acquisition process, on major modification, on platform changes and in cases where expert assistance is required in operational testing and deployment.

(6) Act as the approval authority for the disposal of military exempt lasers.

(7) Maintain documentation of all Navy and Marine Corps laser systems reviewed by the LSRB including all military exempt lasers with the rationale for their exemption.

(8) Report all Navy initiated requests for disposal and transfer of exempted lasers to the Deputy Under Secretary of Defense for Environment and Safety (DUSD (ES)) via Assistant

Secretary of the Navy (Installations and Environment) (ASN(I&E)).

(9) Advise DUSD (ES) via ASN(I&E) of any substantial changes in laser safety policy.

(10) Maintain a current database of ALSOs, TLSOs, LSSs, RLSSs, dates of certification, dates of recertification, and approved instructors.

(11) Establish and publish Navy laser safety design standards and training requirements with input from the LNTL. See reference (g).

(12) Review the ALSO, TLSO, LSS, and RLSS training curricula for approval (in conjunction with the LNTL).

(13) Review personnel and agency qualification to designate qualified instructors for the ALSO, TLSO, LSS, and RLSS courses (in conjunction with the LNTL).

(14) Maintain a list of current LSRB membership.

b. <u>Technical Lead Agent (TLA)</u>. Reference (c) designates the Naval Sea Systems Command (NAVSEASYSCOM) as the TLA for laser safety within the DON. Reference (c) also directs NAVSEASYSCOM to designate the Naval Surface Warfare Center, Dahlgren Division (NSWCDD) Code G73 as the LNTL for laser safety. NAVSEA 04N shall serve as the TLA and, using the technical expertise at NSWCDD Code G73, shall:

(1) Conduct laser safety surveys, measurements, and reviews for all DON lasers and laser installations under the scope of Navy LSRB review. Actual services shall be provided by the LNTL on a cost reimbursable basis.

(2) Represent the DON in tri-service and other interagency laser safety matters and support BUMED in laser radiation medical surveillance.

(3) Maintain membership on national and international standards setting boards and committees to ensure currency of Navy policy.

(4) Evaluate laser ranges and target areas via the Naval Surface Warfare Center, Corona Division, Code SE34, PO Box 5000, Corona, CA 92878, DSN 933-4143, commercial (909) 273-4143 or an ALA/LNTL-approved RLSS.

(5) Evaluate laser protective devices via the Naval Air Warfare Center (NAWC), Aircraft Division (ACDIV), NAWC-ACDIV Vision Laboratory, Code NAVAIR-4.6.7.1, Patuxent River, MD 20670.

(6) Review for approval (in conjunction with the ALA) the ALSO, TLSO, LSS, and RLSS training curricula.

(7) Ensure that LNTL personnel evaluating lasers are LSSs.

c. Laser Safety Review Board (LSRB). The LSRB is an independent authority on laser safety as established by this instruction. The LSRB provides a laser systems safety review of class 3B and 4 lasers used in optical fiber communications systems, all DON lasers used in combat, combat training, or classified in the interest of national security and all laser systems capable of exceeding class 3R levels, except those planned solely for industrial, construction, medical, or indoor experimental laboratory use. This includes systems that are used by other military services and lasers previously registered with the Food and Drug Administration for which modifications in design or use are intended. LSRB review is not required for lasers planned solely for industrial, construction, medical, or indoor experimental laboratory use. The LSRB can act as a source of laser safety guidance for any laser system regardless of its intended use.

(1) The LSRB consists of a permanent and alternate member from all systems commands; BUMED; Headquarters, USMC (Safety Division); the Naval Safety Center; NAWC Aircrew Division; and the LNTL. See enclosure (3).

(2) Enclosures (3) and (4) provide procedures used by the LSRB in its deliberations.

(3) If any facility (including research and development) or procurement office chooses to defer to the LSRB for safety

guidance, the facility shall adhere to the decisions and recommendations of the LSRB.

(4) LSRB approval is limited solely to the laser/laser system and those parts of the testing relating to the laser/ laser system. LSRB review is not intended to be a substitution for a safety or environmental review for all conceivable safety/environmental issues. Final approval for testing or use must come from the appropriate safety manager, environmental and/or occupational health directorate per local instructions.

d. <u>Laser System Acquisition Agent</u>. Commanders of all systems commands, all Navy and Marine Corps program directors and project managers, and research and development activities shall fund and conduct the laser system safety program within their cognizant material support areas. The acquisition agent shall:

(1) Apply system safety methods per reference (h) throughout all life cycle phases of laser systems, laser test fixtures and laser facilities for new systems and modification or different applications of an existing system.

(2) Review the purpose of proposed lasers to determine if they shall meet reference (a) and/or qualify as military exempt. Exempted lasers shall be designed per enclosure (2) and as many of the standards of reference (a) as practical as determined by the LSRB. Substitute control measures (engineering, administrative, or procedural) are required to be as safe as what they are replacing. Lasers that are not classified in the interest of national security that are intended primarily for non-combat training and demonstration, industrial operations, scientific investigations, or medical applications shall not be exempted. Any questions in this regard may be addressed to the LNTL.

(3) Grant exemptions from reference (a) and impose enclosure(2) requirements on manufacturers designing military exempt lasers. Procurement or contracting officers shall grant exemptions to manufacturers in writing and ensure that the system is reviewed by the LSRB. The laser exemption format is given in enclosure (5). A copy of the exemption shall be provided to the ALA.

(4) Ensure that class 3B and class 4 lasers and laser systems and all classes of lasers used for combat, combat training, or are classified in the interest of national security are reviewed by the LSRB. Obtain these reviews before program advancement to the next stage of development, and before test, prototype, or production units are introduced into the Fleet. Resubmit systems for LSRB review when new applications or unapproved platforms are considered. Ensure that operational requirements traceability is demonstrated to the LSRB to prevent proliferation of unnecessary hazardous laser systems. Demonstrate that DoD-approved Laser Eye Protection (LEP) are included in design, planning, training, and use, throughout developmental testing, operational testing, and operational deployment.

(5) Ensure that the LNTL participates in design reviews, evaluates compliance with enclosures (2) and (12), and measures laser output parameters to determine nominal ocular hazard distances, LEP requirements, and other safety related parameters of all lasers prior to review by the LSRB.

(6) Provide the LSRB chair and secretariat safety test data, measurements, laser hazard evaluation results, corrective actions, and other system safety activities conducted per reference (h) and enclosure (4) of this instruction at least 30 days prior to laser reviews.

(7) Implement the requirements of the LSRB.

(8) Ensure DoD-approved laser protective devices are available for operating and maintenance personnel and recommend protection for other personnel or material at risk.

(9) Include all necessary laser safety data in laser technical manuals, maintenance requirement cards, operational manuals, and training curricula.

e. Operational Commands. Navy and Marine Corps commands or activities using class 3B or class 4 lasers, shall:

(1) Establish laser safety organizations per enclosures (6) through (9). A comprehensive operational risk management

program is an essential part of the laser hazard control process and shall be implemented per reference (i).

(2) Impose design and operating requirements of this instruction and enclosure (2) on equipment and facilities. Provide adequate warnings, safety training, documentation, and audits for the control of all hazards resulting from the use of lasers at their activities. Ensure all lasers are classified as to their hazard(s) and labeled per reference (b).

(3) Ensure appropriate LEP is worn by all personnel within the NHZ during testing or operational use of any laser system with the unaided Optical Density (OD) requirement. If optical aids may be used in the exercise, LEP should meet the aided OD requirement.

(4) Appoint the LSSO at that command or activity and forward the LSSO's name, organizational code, and telephone number to the ALA. The activity commander and LSSO will maintain control over laser operations at the local activity.

(5) Ensure that only those laser installations and ranges which have been certified by an RLSS and approved by the activity LSSO as safe for specific applications using specific laser systems are allowed to operate and then solely for those applications. Laser systems shall not be fired outside of these LSSO-designated areas and targets. Technical assistance is available from the LNTL on a cost reimbursable basis to enable commanding officers and their LSSOs to certify the safety of their laser ranges. The commanding officer is responsible for range certification and use per reference (j).

(6) Use and dispose of military exempt lasers per references (c), (k) and (l). Obtain approval of the ALA prior to disposal. The LSRB may be used to ensure that the system is demilitarized per reference (l) or disposed of in accordance with reference (k) that will prevent public access to military exempt technology.

(7) Maintain a current inventory of all military exempt lasers and all class 3B and class 4 lasers as defined in reference (b) for submission to the ALA as requested. A sample format for submission of military exempt laser data is given in

enclosure (10). A sample format for submission of non-military exempt class 3B and class 4 lasers is given in enclosure (11). The LSSO shall keep the inventory of military exempt and class 3B and class 4 lasers. Report lost lasers to the ALA using the inventory formats given in enclosures (10) and (11).

(8) Immediate consultation shall be obtained with an ophthalmologist or optometrist for personnel with suspected or observed laser exposure. Since early medical intervention may lessen the severity of the damage or subsequent retinal scarring for the laser injury, efforts should be made to have the individual promptly seen by an ophthalmologist or at the ophthalmology department of a hospital on an urgent basis. Notify BUMED (M3B4) by electronic mail, fax, message or telephone of suspected or observed laser exposure as soon as possible at commercial (202) 762-3448, DSN 762-3448, fax commercial (202) 762-0931, DSN 762-0931. Additionally, contact the tri-service laser safety hotline (800-473-3549) as soon as possible.

(9) Submit a laser incident report for all cases where personnel are inadvertently exposed to laser energy and maintain the laser incident reports per reference (q) SSIC 8140.1. This report is required for all incidents involving personnel with suspected or observed exposure to class 3B or class 4 lasers. The report shall be sent by the LSSO to BUMED within 30 days of the incident and shall include:

(a) List of personnel involved;

(b) Estimation of laser exposure received to the eyes or skin as related to the applicable MPE per reference (b);

(c) The examining medical officer's immediate and subsequent medical findings (if applicable);

(d) A detailed account of the laser exposure incident. Include the laser's parameters as applicable: wavelength, power or energy, pulse repetition frequency, pulse length, beam size, and divergence;

11

(e) A detailed account of safety procedures and personal protective equipment used at the time of the laser exposure incident; and

(f) Lessons learned and actions completed to prevent another laser exposure incident.

(10) Submit a safety investigation report per references (e), (f), and (g) for all incidents that meet the safety investigation thresholds.

(11) Submit a hazard report for any work-related events that could have potentially resulted in a laser exposure such as using defective safety equipment or inadequate standard operating procedures using the laser incident report criteria in paragraph 7e(9) as applicable.

(12) Obtain LSRB approval for all class 3B, class 4 and military exempt lasers. A laser safety requirements summary is provided in enclosure (12).

(13) Coordinate all space directed (above-horizon) emissions with North American Aerospace Defense Command, CMD/J3S USSTRATCOM JSCC USV, Attn: Orbital Safety Officer, Cheyenne Mountain AFS, CO 80914-6020, Laser Clearinghouse, DSN 268-4416, (719) 474-4416. The following parameters shall be reported: operating wavelength, beam-divergence and output power or energy.

f. Per enclosure (12), Navy and Marine Corps regions, commands, or activities having only class 1, 2, and 3a or 3R lasers not used in combat, combat training or classified in the interest of national security are not required to assign an LSSO. However, they shall:

(1) Ensure users read manufacturer literature and labeling.

(2) Report any instances of contact of the laser beam with an eye to the safety office immediately.

8. Forms and Reports

a. Caution Label, Danger Label, Alternate Danger Label, (shown in Appendix A of enclosure (2)) and Laser Maintenance Area Warning Sign (shown in enclosure (7)) specifications can be located in ANSI Z136.1.

b. Internation Electrotechnical Commission (IEC) Hazard and Explanatory Set of Alternate Labels (shown in Appendix A of enclosure (2)) specifications can be located in ANSI Z136.1 and/or IEC 60825-1.

c. NAVSEA 1995/17, Laser Range Warning Sign, S/N 0118LF0201100, can be ordered from Naval Forms OnLine: https://navalforms.daps.dla.mil/web/public/home.

d. The reporting requirements contained in this instruction are exempt from report control per SECNAV M-5214.1.

R. S. KRAMLICH
Director, Marine Corps Staff

A. M. JOHNSON
Special Assistant for Safety
Matters, Chief of Naval
Operations

Distribution:
Electronic only, via Department of the Navy Issuances Web site
http://doni.daps.dla.mil
MARCORPS PCN 10207270000

LASER SYSTEM SAFETY OFFICER TRAINING REQUIREMENTS

1. <u>General</u>. Laser System Safety Officers (LSSOs) shall have satisfactorily completed a Navy LSSO course. Commands should contact the Administrative Lead Agent (ALA)/Lead Navy Technical Laboratory (LNTL) for the approved formal laser safety course that applies to their situation.

2. <u>Laser System Safety Officers (LSSOs)</u>. There are four categories of LSSOs: ALSO, TLSO, LSS, and RLSS (see definitions below). Retesting at the LSSO's highest certification level is required to maintain certification for all categories of LSSO every 4 years. Recertification exams shall include prerequisite level information. If the LSSO fails the recertification examination, the LSSO will have to be re-certified by attending the appropriate course. Personnel should contact either the ALA or LNTL for recertification testing information. Commanding officers should determine which category of LSSO is appropriate for their commands considering their mission, types of lasers being used, and size of the laser safety program. LSSO categories and qualification descriptions are as follows:

    a. <u>Administrative Laser Safety Officer (ALSO)</u> - The ALSO must successfully complete an ALA/LNTL-approved ALSO course. An ALSO is qualified to:

        (1) Establish and manage a unit level laser safety program.

        (2) Approve, disapprove, or submit for safety approval to higher authority all local laser uses, both portable and fixed.

        (3) Instruct employees and supervisors on the safe use of lasers.

        (4) Supervise laser operations and maintenance.

        (5) Manage laser incident investigations as appropriate. Technical assistance of an LSS or an RLSS is required.

        (6) Maintain a laser medical surveillance program.

        (7) Maintain an inventory of military exempt and class 3B and class 4 lasers.

(8) Post laser warning signs and devices.

(9) Ensure that laser operators have the appropriate knowledge to safely operate their specific lasers (supervisor safety briefs, factory training school, instructional materials, etc.).

(10) Provide safety briefs/pre-mission briefs to laser range users.

(11) Prior to use of a laser range, ensure/confirm that warning signs have been posted, the area is clear of specular reflectors, personnel have required Laser Eye Protection (LEP), and all other safety conditions for range laser use outlined in the range regulations or range standard operating procedures (SOPs) are met.

(12) Perform LEP inspections.

b. <u>Technical Laser Safety Officer (TLSO)</u> - A TLSO must successfully complete an ALA/LNTL-approved TLSO course. A TLSO is qualified to:

(1) Understand the calculations and measurements of laser safety parameters such as Nominal Ocular Hazard Distances (NOHDs) and required Optical Densities (ODs) for laser eyewear.

(2) Train ALSOs using the ALA-approved course curriculum (qualification of TLSOs as instructors requires ALA/LNTL approval).

(3) Understand classification of lasers and laser systems.

(4) Perform the duties of a laboratory, installation, base, research facility, or Range Laser Safety Officer (RLSO) as follows:

(a) Establish and manage a base or installation laser range safety program.

(b) Approve/disapprove the use of laser systems and/or any laser operations on their range that fall within the guidelines of the range certification.

          (c) Perform annual range safety compliance inspections to include:

              <u>1</u>. Verification of range boundary warning signs;

              <u>2</u>. Target conditions;

              <u>3</u>. Accessibility and condition of ground laser system firing points; and

              <u>4</u>. Other laser safety controls, as appropriate.

          (d) Ensure laser ranges under their cognizance are certified/recertified by an RLSS at least every 3 years or when changes to the range fall outside the current certification.

          (e) Ensure range regulations/SOPs are provided to commands requesting usage of the laser range.

          (f) Review the training plan (to include laser type(s) and proposed employment tactics) of each command requesting access to the laser range to ensure compliance with current laser range certification.

      (5) Perform the same duties as an ALSO.

   c. <u>Laser Safety Specialist (LSS)</u>. The LSS must successfully complete the ALA/LNTL-approved LSS course. An LSS is qualified to:

      (1) Perform the calculations and measurements of laser safety parameters such as NOHDs and required ODs for laser eyewear.

      (2) Train ALSOs, TLSOs, RLSOs, and LSSs using the ALA-approved course curriculum. (Qualification of instructors requires ALA/LNTL approval.)

      (3) Classify lasers and laser systems.

      (4) Conduct technical aspects of laser incident investigations.

      (5) Perform the same tasks as a TLSO.

d. <u>Range Laser Safety Specialist (RLSS)</u>. An RLSS must successfully complete an ALA/LNTL-approved RLSS course. An RLSS is qualified to:

(1) Conduct laser radiation hazard surveys and evaluations for commanding officer approval of certification.

(2) Perform the calculations and measurements required to certify a laser range.

(3) Train ALSOs and RLSSs using the ALA-approved course curriculum. Qualification of instructors requires ALA/LNTL approval.

(4) Conduct technical aspects of laser range incident investigations.

(5) Perform the same tasks as a TLSO.

LASER SAFETY DESIGN REQUIREMENT CHECKLISTS

The checklists in this enclosure are intended to help the designer, procuring activity, or personnel responsible for laser safety stay within the laser safety design requirements for military lasers and associated support equipment. There may be requirements where the wording may not precisely apply to the particular situation; therefore, some individual interpretation of the requirements is necessary. Because each individual's interpretation of the requirements may differ, room has been made available to expand upon the answer to each requirement. The checklists should not be used by themselves, but in conjunction with other references (e.g., MIL-STD-882D[1] and ANSI Z136.1[2]).

EQUIPMENT DESCRIPTION

Equipment Name:_____

System Name to be Used
throughout Approval and Use:_____

Documented Operational Requirements
for Laser Use:_____

Model Number: _____ Serial Number: _____

Manufacturer: _____

Address: _____

_____

Responsible Authority:_____

Address: _____

_____

Point of Contact: _____

Address: _____

_____

Phone: _____

Inspector: _____ Date: _____

---

[1]MIL-STD-882D, *Department of Defense Standard Practice for System Safety,* 2000.
[2]ANSI Z136.1, *American National Standard Institute Safe Use of Lasers,* 2007.

APPENDIX A

LASER DESIGN REQUIREMENT CHECKLIST

Item	Requirement	Yes/No	Comment
1	Is laser product provided with a tag or label permanently affixed to the device housing?		
1a	Does such a tag or label contain the full name and address of the manufacturer, the laser model, and the place, month, and year of manufacture?		
1b	Is label or tag information not expressed in code?		
2	In lieu of the certification label required by 21 Code of Federal Regulations (CFR) 1010.2; if laser is product exempted under 76EL-01 Department of Defense (DoD), is a tag or label permanently affixed to the device housing so that it is readily accessible to view?		
2a	Does such a tag or label contain the following statement? **CAUTION** **This electronic product has been exempted from FDA radiation safety performance standards prescribed in Title 21, CFR, chapter I, subchapter J, under Exemption No. 76EL-01 DoD issued on 26 July 1976. This product should not be used without adequate protective devices or procedures.**		
3	Are laser products operational and adjustment controls located so that human exposure to laser radiation in excess of the appropriate Maximum Permissible Exposure (MPE) is unnecessary for the operation or adjustment of such controls?		
4	Is laser product designed to preclude unintentional laser output (e.g., spontaneous firing)?		

Item	Requirement	Yes/No	Comment
5	Are lasers and associated optics designed so that external secondary beams are not generated unless necessary for the performance of the intended function(s)?		
6	Are focused beams, hot spots, and collateral radiation minimized?		
7	Do lasers employing frequency shifting or harmonic multipliers reduce unnecessary emissions below MPE?		
8	Is the laser system designed to preclude unintentional self-oscillation, mode-locking, double-pulsing, or unwanted modes, when practicable?		
9	If unwanted modes cannot be eliminated, is laser classified as per the worst possible accessible emission level?		
10	Are interlocked protective housings provided to protect personnel from high-voltage sources and unnecessary laser and collateral radiation in excess of the Accessible Emission Limits (AELs)?		
10a	Is aural or visual indication of interlock defeat provided?		
10b	Do interlocks return to their normal operation when access cover or door is returned?		
11	When laser radiation exceeding American National Standard Institute (ANSI) AEL for class 1 is accessible, are visual indicators readily visible while wearing suitable laser protective eyewear?		
12	Do viewing ports and display screens, which allow the operator to view laser radiation, attenuate the radiation to limit personnel exposure to below the appropriate MPE?		

Item	Requirement	Yes/No	Comment
13	Do laser product pointing or viewing optics having a magnifying power exceeding 1.0 include a built-in laser safety filter within the optical train that protects the operator from reflections from specular surfaces or exposures from force-on-force training?		
13a	Is adequate visibility maintained when using laser safety filters?		
13b	Are laser safety filters permanently attached or designed so that the optical train cannot be assembled without the filter?		
13c	Is filter on viewing sight marked to indicate optical density (OD)& wavelength?		
14	Is there a label marking the output aperture?		
15	**Items 15-22 are class 1, 1M 2, 2M, or 3R laser requirements** Do laser warning labels for exempted lasers provide clear instructions to the operators, maintainers, and potential bystanders to preclude laser injury?		
16	Do lasers classified as ANSI class 1, class 2, or class 3R meet the design (performance) requirements of 21 CFR class 1, class 2, respectively, except where such requirements restrict operational capability or security?		
17	Do lasers classified as ANSI Class 1, class 2, or class 3A or 3R meet the designation and warning requirements of 21 CFR class 1 and class 2, respectively, with the exception that the ANSI classification will be displayed in the lower right corner rather than the Food and Drug Administration (FDA) class?		

Item	Requirement	Yes/No	Comment
18	Are labels permanently affixed or inscribed on such products as to be legible and readily accessible to view when the product is fully assembled for use?		
19	Are warning labels affixed to the laser system housing near the beam exit port and/or fire button when possible in such a manner that viewing the label does not require personnel exposure to laser radiation?		
20	Are class 2 or some 3R lasers, as defined by ANSI, provided with a label similar to the examples illustrated in figures 2-1 or 2-3?		
20a	Is numerical output information [e.g., wavelength(s) and maximum power output (when unclassified)] located along the lower edge in a smaller font?		
20b	Does the word **INVISIBLE** or **VISIBLE**, as appropriate, precede the word **RADIATION**?		
20c	When labels may compromise camouflage, are muted colors appropriate to the camouflage paint scheme used?		
20d	Is information classified in the interest of national security omitted from all labels?		
21	When a laser has a defeatable interlock that, when defeated, allows access to class 3B or class 4 emission levels, is an additional label that states the following installed on or near the access panel? **DANGER** **Laser Radiation When Open and Interlock Defeated, Avoid Eye or Skin Exposure to Direct or Scattered Radiation.**		

Item	Requirement	Yes/No	Comment
22	If non-exempted lasers incorporate military labeling, has alternate labeling been requested by the manufacturer and approved as a variance by the FDA in accordance with 21 CFR 1040 (g) (10)?		
23	**Items 23-43 are Class 3B and Class 4 laser design requirements** Are class 3B, class 4, and some 3R lasers, as defined by ANSI, provided with a label similar to the examples illustrated in figures 2-2a, 2-2b, or 2-3?		
23a	Are such labels permanently affixed or inscribed on such products to be legible and readily accessible to view when the product is fully assembled for use?		
23b	Is the label affixed to the laser system housing near the fire button and exit port when the port is remote from the operator in such a manner that viewing the label does not require personnel exposure to laser radiation?		
23c	Does the label use the word **DANGER** and include the type of laser and the word **VISIBLE** or **INVISIBLE** preceding the word **RADIATION**?		

Item	Requirement	Yes/No	Comment
23d	Does the label contain an appropriate instructional safety statement or control message for the operator or bystander as applicable? For class 3B and class 4 ground target designators: **DO NOT AIM AT PERSONNEL OR FLAT GLASS SURFACES** For class 4 lasers that present a diffuse reflection hazard: **DO NOT AIM AT PERSONNEL OR FLAT GLASS SURFACES OR TARGETS WITHIN __ METERS** Bystander warning for wavelengths 400 to 1400 nm; class 3B and class 4 lasers: **DO NOT LOOK INTO PORTHOLE** Bystander warning for wavelengths 1400 nm to 1 mm and 180 to 400 nm; class 3B and class 4 lasers: **DO NOT EXPOSE EYE OR SKIN TO DIRECT OR SPECULARLY REFLECTED BEAMS**		
23e	Do **DANGER** labels have **DANGER** printed upon a white background with a bright red oval around the word **DANGER** and contain a red starburst and black lettering?		
23f	When camouflage may be compromised by such warning labels, are appropriate muted colors (i.e., olive drab) used?		
23g	If the information is unclassified, are the ANSI laser hazard classification, wavelength(s), and maximum radiant power or energy added along the lower edge of the label?		

Item	Requirement	Yes/No	Comment
24	Are measures taken to prevent single operator or material error causing unintentional laser output that exceeds ANSI AEL for class 1?		
25	Are at least two operator actions (one of which shall serve as a laser arming control) required to cause the laser to function?		
26	Is laser output impossible when arming control is in the safe position?		
27	Is the laser fire trigger or switch clearly identified and physically protected to prevent accidental activation (when possible, the switch shall be a guarded positive action type that requires continuous operator intent to operate the laser product and laser output shall cease immediately upon release)?		
28	If the laser is a single-pulsed laser, is the activation circuitry designed so that continual depression or short-circuiting of the fire control switch will not cause repeated emissions [unless necessary for the performance of intended function(s)]?		
29	If operational considerations preclude the use of a dead-man switch, a toggled switch may be used if adequate design safeguards are provided to prevent long-term inadvertent lasing (e.g., through a watchdog timer and/or system logic switching device). Are these employed?		
30	Does the laser have a permanently installed/attached exit port cover that prevents access by any part of the body to all laser radiation in excess of ANSI AEL for class 1?		

Item	Requirement	Yes/No	Comment
30a	Does the cover chosen clearly indicate that it is in place (safe) or open?		
30b	Is the cover designed to withstand repeated laser firings when it is in either position?		
31	Is a readily available remote-control interlock capability incorporated on the laser or auxiliary power supply systems?		
31a	Does the remote control connector have an electrical potential no greater than 130 root mean squared volts between terminals (not essential if the laser is always directed into an interlocked set enclosure for maintenance or service procedures)?		
31b	When the terminals of the connector are not electrically joined, is human access to all laser radiation and collateral radiation in excess of ANSI AEL for class 1 prevented?		
31c	Is an intentional reset needed to reactivate the system once disconnected?		
32	Is the boresight alignment and retention designed consistent with system mission requirements (considered a safety-critical item)?		
33	Are laser status (emission) indicators (aural or visual or as specified by the procuring agency) provided to inform the operator when the laser is prepared to fire (armed) and when the laser is actually firing?		
33a	If visual indicators are used for operation or maintenance, are they visible during daylight, nighttime, and when viewed through appropriate protective eye wear?		

Item	Requirement	Yes/No	Comment
33b	Are indicators located so that viewing does not require personnel exposure to laser radiation in excess of the ANSI AEL for class 1?		
34	Is there a means to differentiate between armed and firing (e.g., continuous tone or light is armed and intermittent tone or blinking light is firing)?		
35	If the laser system is installed on an aircraft, is it designed to prevent laser output while the aircraft is not airborne?		
35a	Is an override switch for ground maintenance designed to prevent inadvertent activation?		
36	Does the laser product incorporate controls to optimize positive operator control of beam pointing?		
36a	Does it include a means of ensuring boresight retention and software systems safety?		
37	For systems with automatic target tracking capability, is an automatic disable capacity incorporated to inhibit laser firing if target tracking outside the system specifications occurs or when the laser sight line reaches the gimbal limits or the system mask limit?		
38	If no hardware stops are installed, are at least two independent systems capable of disabling the laser (a provision to override these automatic features during combat is permitted)?		

Item	Requirement	Yes/No	Comment
39	For lasers using a beam scanning technique, if irregularities not normal to the operation and unintended pattern changes increase the hazard potential of the laser product, does it include a feature that terminates or reduces the beam output to ANSI AEL for class 1 immediately upon the cessation of scanning irregularities (change in either scan velocity or amplitude)?		
40	If a training mode is required for the laser, are provisions made (beam attenuator, expander, diffuser or less-hazardous lasers, TV cameras, etc.) to reduce hazardous emissions to the lowest level consistent with training requirements?		
41	If the laser can be used in both a mission and a training mode, is a visual indication provided to inform the operator and outside observers that the laser is positively in the training mode?		
42	Have the system's Nominal Ocular Hazard Distance (NOHD), skin hazard distance, diffuse reflection hazard determination, protective eye wear requirements, buffer zone requirements, and safety parameters been certified by measurements by Naval Surface Warfare Center Dahlgren Division (NSWCDD) (Code G73) and approved by the Laser Safety Review Board (LSRB)?		
43	Do aiming optics employ a reticle that can be viewed under any illumination conditions?		
43a	Does the reticle not impair dark adaptation of observer's eyes?		
43b	Is the reticle calibrated so the operator can determine the proximity of the laser beam to target buffer zones?		

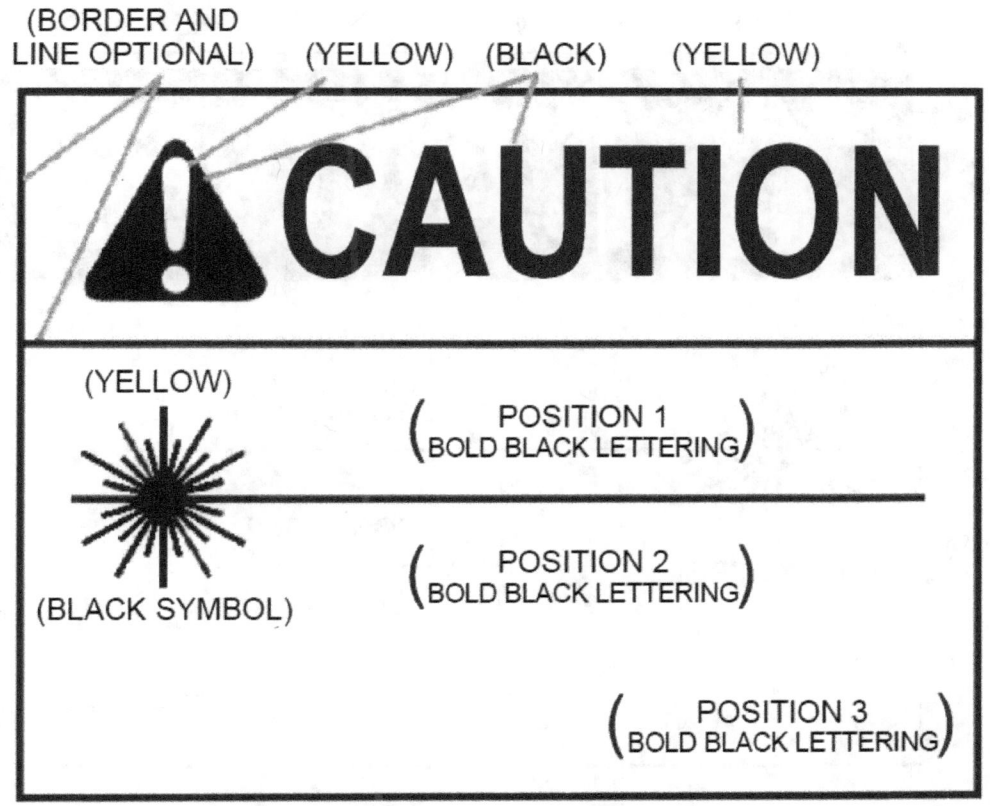

FIGURE 2-1. EXAMPLE OF A CAUTION LABEL. At position 1, precautionary information should be provided, such as "Do not stare into the beam." At position 2, the type of laser should be provided, such as "Helium Neon," and at position 3, the hazard class of the laser should be provided. Below the starburst, additional information on the characteristics of the laser should be provided such as laser wavelength and pulse characteristics.

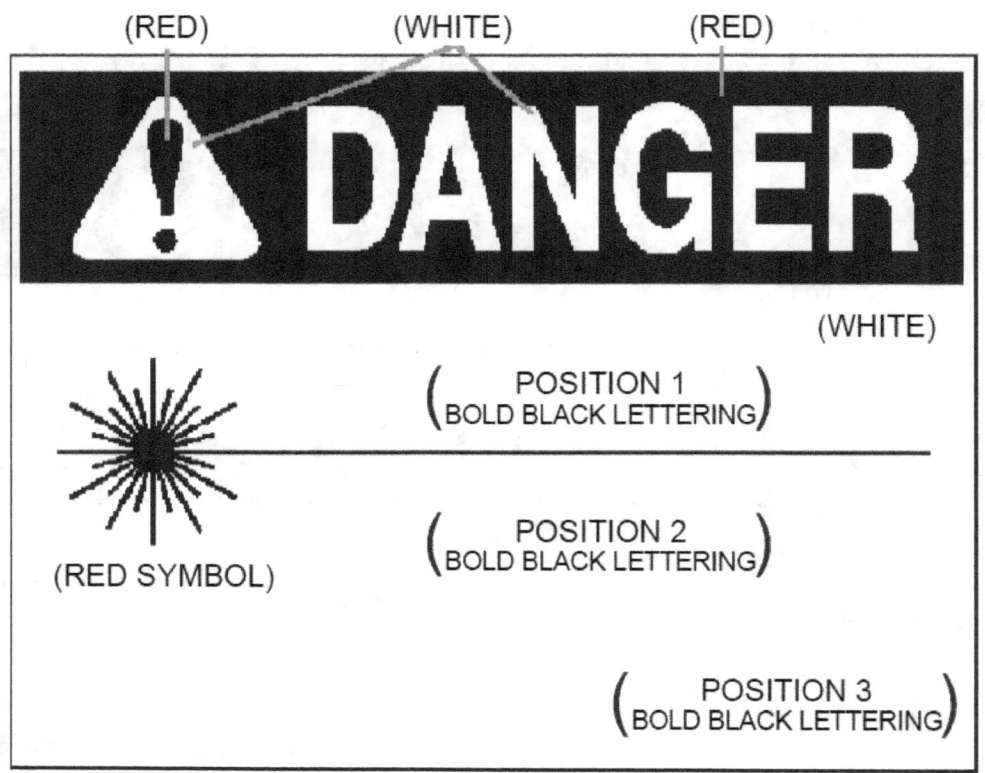

FIGURE 2-2a.   EXAMPLE OF A DANGER LABEL.   Starburst is red;
letters are black.   Precautions including the NOHD would be
placed above the tail of the starburst at position 1.   The type
of laser, including output power, pulse characteristics, and
whether the output is visible or invisible, is placed below the
tail of the starburst at position 2.   The ANSI classification is
placed in the lower right hand corner at position 3.

FIGURE 2-2b.   EXAMPLE OF AN ALTERNATE DANGER LABEL.   Starburst
is red; letters are black.   Precautions including the NOHD would
be placed above the tail of the starburst. The type of laser,
including output power or pulse characteristics, is placed below
the starburst.   If the output of the laser is invisible, the
word "invisible" should be included below the tail of the
starburst.   The ANSI classification is placed in the lower right
hand corner.

SYMBOL AND BORDER: BLACK
BACKGROUND: YELLOW

SPACE FOR LEGEND

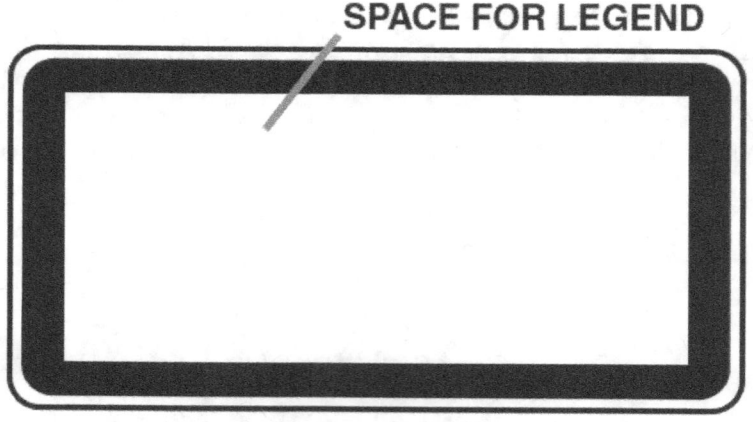

LEGEND AND BORDER: BLACK
BACKGROUND: YELLOW

FIGURE 2-3. EXAMPLE OF AN INTERNATIONAL ELECTROTECHNICAL
COMMISSION(IEC) HAZARD AND EXPLANATORY SET OF ALTERNATE LABELS.
Starburst and borders are black; backgrounds are yellow.
Explanations on the explanatory label shall be commensurate with
the class of laser being labeled. Examples of explanatory
statements can be found in ANSI Z136.1 and/or IEC 60825-1.

APPENDIX B

SUPPORT EQUIPMENT DESIGN REQUIREMENT CHECKLIST

Item	Requirement	Yes/No	Comment
1	**Items 1-7 are applicable to all classes of laser support equipment** If the laser support equipment is military exempt, is it used solely in support of exempted lasers?		
2	Is the laser support equipment designed to ensure that laser radiation emitted during maintenance or service is no greater than the ANSI AEL for class 1 and that collateral radiation is not in excess of applicable limits, when practicable?		
3	Does the equipment confine the laser radiation within an opaque enclosure?		
4	Is the enclosure interlocked to prevent exposure to levels in excess of the ANSI AEL for class 1 when the enclosure is removed?		
5	Is the enclosure provided with the appropriate exterior warning indicators and labels?		
6	Have other associated hazards been addressed and controlled by suitable engineering programs per Military Standard (MIL-STD)-882 (NOTAL), MIL-STD-2036 (NOTAL)?		
7	Are adequate instructions as to safe techniques and personnel protective means included in all technical manuals and plainly marked on the laser product when potentially hazardous areas are accessible?		

Item	Requirement	Yes/No	Comment
8	**Items 8-13 are applicable to class 1, 1M, 2, 2M, or 3R laser support equipment requirements** Does the laser support equipment meet the design (performance) requirements of 21 CFR class 1, class 2, or class 3R, respectively, except where such requirements restrict operational capability or security?		
9	Does the laser support equipment meet designation and warning requirements of 21 CFR class 1, class 2, or class 3R, respectively, with the exception that the ANSI classification will be displayed in the lower right corner rather than the FDA class?		
10	Are labels permanently affixed or inscribed on such products as to be legible and readily accessible to view when the product is fully assembled for use?		
11	Are warning labels affixed to the housing in such a manner that viewing the label does not require personnel exposure to laser radiation?		
11a	Is numerical output information [e.g., wavelength(s) and maximum power output (when unclassified)] located along the lower edge in a smaller font?		
11b	Does the word **INVISIBLE** or **VISIBLE**, as appropriate, precede the word **RADIATION**?		
11c	When labels may compromise camouflage, are muted colors appropriate to the camouflage paint scheme used?		
11d	Is information classified in the interest of national security omitted from labels?		

Item	Requirement	Yes/No	Comment
12	When a laser has a defeatable interlock that, when defeated, allows access to class 3B or class 4 emission levels, is an additional label that states the following installed on or near the access panel? **DANGER** **Laser Radiation When Open and Interlock Defeated, Avoid Eye or Skin Exposure to Direct or Scattered Radiation.**		
13	Does non-exempted support equipment incorporate military labeling when alternate labeling has been requested by the manufacturer and approved as a variance by the FDA in accordance with 21 CFR 1040 (g)(10)?		
14	**Items 14-24 are class 3B and class 4 laser support equipment requirements** Does the laser system test equipment for boresight and laser performance testing attenuate the beam to limit personnel exposure to below AEL for ANSI class 1?		
15	Is the laser system test equipment for boresight and laser performance testing interlocked to the laser to prevent inadvertent laser operation outside the enclosure if the test equipment is not used in a closed installation?		
16	Is an access interlock switch interfaced with ANSI class 3B and class 4 laser systems under test such that inadvertent removal of test sets or poor connection will terminate or limit the laser output to the ANSI AEL for class 1 or class 2, if applicable?		

Item	Requirement	Yes/No	Comment
17	Is a warning system activated immediately prior to operation of the laser and remain activated until the laser output has been reduced to the ANSI AEL for class 1 or class 2, if applicable?		
17a	Is the warning system designed not to attract personnel attention in such a manner as to create a potential hazard?		
18	Does all support equipment for laser hardware that could directly activate the laser preferably incorporate a positive action (dead-man) switch that must be activated when laser firing is desired?		
19	When a dead-man switch is not incorporated, is an emergency cutoff switch provided that allows emergency cutoff of laser output in excess of ANSI AEL for class 1 or class 2, as appropriate?		
19a	Is the switch readily accessible from the operator's position and permit one-step operation?		
20	Is a key-lock master switch provided to prevent unauthorized activation of any test facility component used to supply power directly to the laser that is necessary for its operation?		
21	Is the laser beam terminated by a beam stop that is diffuse (i.e., has a low value of reflectance at the laser wavelength)?		
21a	Is such a beam stop fire resistant and unable to emit toxic or carcinogenic fumes when exposed to the laser(s) for which it was designed?		
21b	Is the beam stop marked for the type(s) and power level(s) of laser(s) for which it is procured?		

Item	Requirement	Yes/No	Comment
22	Are appropriate control measures for the protection of personnel (e.g., appropriate exhaust ventilation) provided where toxic gases cannot be prevented, such as firebrick, which contains beryllium compounds?		
23	Are class 3B and class 4 laser support equipment, as defined by ANSI, provided with a label similar to the examples illustrated in figures 2-2a and 2-2b?		
23a	Are such labels permanently affixed or inscribed on such products to be legible and readily accessible to view when the product is fully assembled for use?		
23b	Is the label affixed to the laser system housing near the fire button and exit port when the port is remote from the operator in such a manner that viewing the label does not require personnel exposure to laser radiation?		
23c	Does the label use the word **DANGER** and include the type of laser and the word **VISIBLE** or **INVISIBLE** preceding the word **RADIATION**?		
23d	Does the label contain an appropriate instructional safety statement or control message for the operator or bystander as applicable? For class 3B and class 4 ground target designators: **DO NOT AIM AT PERSONNEL OR FLAT GLASS SURFACES**		

Item	Requirement	Yes/No	Comment
23d Con.	For class 4 laser support equipment that present a diffuse reflection hazard: **DO NOT AIM AT PERSONNEL OR FLAT GLASS SURFACES OR TARGETS WITHIN ___ METERS** Bystander warning for wavelengths 400 to 1400 nm; class 3B and class 4 laser support equipment **DO NOT LOOK INTO PORTHOLE** Bystander warning for wavelengths 1400 nm to 1 mm and 180 to 400 nm; class 3B and class 4 laser support equipment: **DO NOT EXPOSE EYE OR SKIN TO DIRECT OR SPECULARLY REFLECTED BEAMS**		
23e	Do **DANGER** labels have **DANGER** printed upon a white background with a bright red oval around the word **DANGER** and contain a red starburst and black lettering?		
23f	When camouflage may be compromised by such warning labels, are appropriate muted colors (i.e., olive drab) used?		
23g	If the information is unclassified, are the ANSI laser hazard classification, wavelength(s), and maximum radiant power or energy added along the lower edge of the label?		
24	Is laser output impossible when arming control is in the safe position?		

APPENDIX C

LASER FACILITY DESIGN REQUIREMENT CHECKLIST

Item	Requirement	Yes/No	Comment
1	Is support equipment designed such that laser radiation emitted during maintenance or service is no greater than the ANSI AEL for class 1 and collateral radiation is not in excess of applicable limits when practicable?		
2	Can support equipment confine the laser radiation within an enclosure that is adequately interlocked to prevent levels in excess of ANSI AEL for class 1 when the enclosure is removed?		
2a	Is the enclosure provided with appropriate exterior warning indicators and labels?		
3	Have other associated hazards been addressed and controlled by suitable engineering programs per MIL-STD-882, MIL-STD-2036, and ANSI Z136.1?		
4	Are adequate instructions as to safe techniques and personnel protective means included in all technical references (manuals) and plainly marked on the laser product when potentially hazardous areas are accessible?		
5	Is facility designed for limited personnel access?		
6	Is facility a closed installation for class 3B and class 4 lasers?		
7	Are reasonably high illumination levels at the work areas attainable to overcome any reduction in visual performance primarily due to the use of laser protective eyewear?		
8	When practicable, is facility designed so that no personal protective equipment is required?		

Item	Requirement	Yes/No	Comment
9	When the hands or other parts of the body are likely to be exposed to potentially hazardous levels, are protective coverings provided?		
10	Are all personnel working in laser facility provided with suitable personal protective clothing and equipment?		
11	Does laser protective eyewear provide complete protection for the individual's field-of-view and is it marked with the optical density (OD) at the specific laser wavelengths?		
12	Is protective eyewear selected according to the laser equipment used at that facility?		
13	Is protective eyewear selected suitable for individuals requiring corrective lenses as well as for uncorrected vision?		
14	**Items 14-26 are applicable to class 3B and class 4 laser facility requirements** Is a laser warning sign displayed on all entry points or doors to the facility?		
14a	Do warning signs use the word **DANGER** and include the type of laser (**VISIBLE** and/or **INVISIBLE**), as appropriate, and precede the word **RADIATION**?		
14b	Do such warning signs contain an appropriate instructional statement; e.g., **KNOCK BEFORE ENTERING** or **KNOCK AND WAIT**?		
15	Are access interlock switches interfaced with ANSI class 3B and class 4 laser systems under test such that inadvertent entry into facility will terminate or limit the laser output to the ANSI AEL for class 1 or class 2?		

Item	Requirement	Yes/No	Comment
15a	Are these interlock systems such that inadvertent removal or poor connection of test sets will terminate or limit laser output to ANSI AEL class 1 or class 2?		
16	Is a warning system, external to the facility, activated immediately prior to operation of the laser and remain activated until laser output has been reduced to the ANSI AEL for class 1 or class 2, if applicable?		
17	Does the facility incorporate operation switches and beam stops per checklist items 24 through 26 for support equipment requirements?		
18	Does test equipment for boresight and laser performance enclose the beam to limit personnel exposure to below class 1 AEL?		
19	Is test equipment interlocked to laser to prevent inadvertent laser operation outside the enclosure if test is not in a closed installation?		
20	Where the laser is not otherwise supported rigidly, is a mechanical fixture provided to rigidly attach the laser in a fixed position during testing and maintenance?		
21	Are location & orientation of test fixtures such that exposure of personnel to direct beam is minimized?		
22	Are the interior surfaces of the facility painted with a finish that has a low value of reflectance at the laser wavelength(s) and that will diffuse the laser beam while maintaining an acceptable ambient illumination?		

Item	Requirement	Yes/No	Comment
23	Are additional safety features to warn personnel to clear the beam path area and a low-power visible laser subsystem for pre-alignment provided?		
24	If the facility is designed for very high-power continuous wave (CW) or pulsed lasers, does it have a means to enclose the entire beam path within the facility?		
24a	Is the enclosure designed to withstand the direct beam?		
25	If necessary, are remote-control firing and television monitoring provided?		
26	Have associated hazards been controlled? Have ANSI Z136.1 guidelines been considered?		

APPENDIX D

LASER PROTECTIVE EYEWEAR CHECKLIST

Item	Requirement	Yes/No	Comment
1	Are the laser wavelength and protection level covered by a DoD approved Laser Eye Protective (LEP) device available to the laser operator and maintainer?		
2	Does laser protective eyewear protect against the worst possible exposure situation?		
3	Does it allow the best compromise between protection and high visibility?		
4	Is protective eyewear fully compatible with normal corrective lenses (spectacles)?		
5	Does protective eyewear take into consideration all hazardous wavelengths emitted from the laser?		
6	Is wavelength range for which eyewear is designed clearly marked on the protective eyewear?		
7	Is the OD at each wavelength for which the protective eyewear is designed clearly marked on the eyewear?		
8	Is user information for LEP provided?		
9	Is the damage threshold of approved LEP in excess of the maximum output emitted by the laser?		
10	Is the protective eyewear durable for the anticipated environment and lifetime?		
11	Has protective eyewear with curved lenses been considered?		
12	Is protective eyewear in good condition, i.e., no scratches, pits, or cracks?		
13	If relying on commercial LEP, has the manufacturer provided laser testing results?		

**REQUIREMENTS AND PROCEDURES OF THE
LASER SAFETY REVIEW BOARD (LSRB)**

1. <u>Laser Safety Review Board</u>. The LSRB ensures that laser safety criteria are incorporated in all Department of Navy (DON) laser systems capable of creating eye injury and other lasers eligible for military exemption from reference (a) used in the DON. The LSRB membership shall elect a chair every 2 years. The chair should be a qualified Laser Safety Specialist (LSS). The Administrative Lead Agent (ALA) shall provide the secretariat and administrative support.

2. <u>Scope</u>. The LSRB shall review all lasers and laser systems used for combat, combat training, or classified in the interest of national security (not designed solely for medical or indoor experimental laboratory use) to determine the potential hazards of the lasers, especially with respect to laser radiation, during all phases of development, use, maintenance, transportation, storage and disposal. All lasers capable of exceeding the accessible exposure limits or maximum permissible exposure limits for a class 3A or class 3R laser require review by the LSRB, with the exception of lasers used solely in industrial or medical settings.

3. <u>Composition</u>. The LSRB is an independent authority on laser safety as established by this instruction. All systems commands, the Bureau of Medicine and Surgery, Marine Corps Headquarters (SD), the Naval Safety Center, the technical lead agent, and the Lead Navy Technical Laboratory (LNTL) shall provide a permanent and alternate member to the LSRB. The names, telephone numbers of the members, and their security clearances shall be forwarded to the ALA. Members of the LSRB shall be technical laser safety officers. There should be at least one range laser safety specialist on the LSRB and the technical laboratory members shall be LSSs. The ALA shall provide a permanent secretary for the LSRB. Personnel assigned as members of the LSRB shall be experienced in laser safety and have no responsibility for the development or effectiveness of the item under review. Designated LSRB members should seek assistance in technical documentation review either from the program manager, the laser system contractor, or the LNTL when needed.

4. <u>Responsibilities</u>. The LSRB shall review the hazardous aspects of each laser system presented to ensure that all safety requirements including design features, procedures, precautions

and training are included in the laser installation and documentation. Having established the degree of safety incorporated in the laser system, the LSRB, through the chair, renders a judgment as to the safety of the system and presents its requirements and recommendations regarding the advancement of the system to the next stage of the acquisition life cycle. The LSRB members shall have a current SECRET clearance for classified meetings. Specific responsibilities are as follows:

    a. <u>The chair of the LSRB shall</u>:

        (1) Convene the LSRB as deemed necessary when requested by the program office or systems command.

        (2) Preside at LSRB meetings.

        (3) Ensure implementation of LSRB functions.

        (4) Issue LSRB requirements and recommendations to the responsible agent for each laser presented within 30 days of the meeting.

    b. <u>The secretariat shall</u>:

        (1) Coordinate with the chair to schedule LSRB meetings as required.

        (2) Provide administrative support to the LSRB.

        (3) Issue reports generated by the LSRB.

        (4) Maintain the official files of the LSRB per reference (r). Marine Corps records shall be maintained per reference (s).

        (5) Maintain an archive or record all electronic mail (e-mail) messages/ message traffic resulting from informal LSRB meetings per reference (r). Marine Corps records shall be maintained per reference (s).

        (6) Maintain an LSRB charter that has the consensus of its membership and has been signed by the current chair of the LSRB.

c. Members shall:

(1) Review technical documents presented prior to LSRB meetings.

(2) Render an independent appraisal of the laser safety aspects along with a recommendation concerning safety approval of the item under review. All phases of the life cycle are to be considered, with emphasis given to the life cycle phases of specific concern to the command represented.

(3) Ensure that the LSRB secretariat receives copies of all e-mail messages resulting from informal LSRB meetings.

d. All Navy and Marine Corps program/project managers and commanding officers of facilities with lasers shall:

(1) Submit all items within the scope of this instruction for LSRB review at appropriate times throughout the entire life cycle (concept and technology development, system development and demonstration, production and deployment, and sustainment and disposal).

(2) Submit a document package per enclosure (4), for review at least 30 days prior to the established meeting date to the LSRB chair and secretariat. The document package shall be sent to each member of the LSRB. LSRB addresses will be supplied by the ALA or LNTL upon request and can be found on the Navy Laser Safety Website at http://www.navylasersafety.com.

(3) Ensure that the LNTL is provided with funding and the required device information to perform the laser safety survey, measurements, and review of the laser system at least two weeks prior to the LSRB meeting.

5. Scheduling. Reviews of proposed systems shall be scheduled well in advance of any use of the laser or laser system so that LSRB requirements and recommendations can be implemented prior to use. The evaluation shall be scheduled with the LNTL at least 30 days prior to the desired date of the evaluation.

**GUIDELINES FOR SUBMISSION OF A LASER DATA PACKAGE
AND PRESENTATION AT THE LASER SAFETY REVIEW BOARD (LSRB) MEETING**

1. The content of the document package and the presentation is mainly affected by three considerations:

    a. The complexity of the item to be presented;

    b. The point in the life cycle in which the review is conducted; and

    c. The security classification of the material.

2. The following guidelines will assist in preparing for the LSRB. Advice and assistance may be sought from the secretariat of the LSRB and the Lead Navy Technical Laboratory (LNTL). Systems reviewed later in their life cycle and more complex systems typically require a voluminous data package for review.

    a. Documentation should be sufficiently complete and detailed to allow a meaningful review of all laser safety aspects by LSRB members prior to the presentation. Information shall not exceed the SECRET level. It should completely describe:

        (1) The design of the system. A full set of design drawings is not desired, but rather documents such as assembly drawings, firing circuits, or other sketches that would indicate or assist in describing the system. Emphasis should be put on components, hardware, software, and human factors affecting safety.

        (2) The operation of the system. A concise but thorough description of the intended use of the system including maintenance, boresight determination and error, boresight retention, calculated and measured tracking and aiming accuracy, storage areas, use environment, handling equipment, laser platform, platform stability, performance sequence, disposal methods, etc.

        (3) The safety features of the system. Describe the system safety program plan and its results including a list of all types and scopes of hazard analyses. Observations made during development, test, and evaluation of the system and support equipment (such as protective devices) that bear on laser safety should be presented. All safety devices

incorporated in the system as well as precautionary measures to be invoked, such as the methods of beam stop control and establishment of cutouts, are to be identified. Also required is a description of the extent to which the system meets the requirements of applicable standards, specifications, and safety controls.

(4) The documentation and training support for the system. Include laser custodian information, laser identification/type designation, contract number, national stock number and location(s), and number of lasers. Verify that the required publication and training programs are being or have been developed to assure the safe operation, training, handling, transportation, storage, and disposal of the laser system.

b. The major theme of the presentation should be the system safety program results with design and operation being covered in depth. While a definite time limit cannot be established, it is suggested that the presentation be limited to two hours. The persons most familiar with the system safety program and the design and operation of the system should give the presentation. Naval Surface Warfare Center, Dahlgren Division (NSWCDD), Code G73, will present their findings at the LSRB meeting provided their evaluation has been completed. Contact the LSRB chair or secretariat regarding audiovisual requirements at least 2 weeks prior to the meeting. Attendees at the presentation should include the program manager, the system engineer, the laser system safety officer, and a user of the system from the Fleet, squadron, etc.

c. The LNTL or its designee will perform all measurements for hazard determination to be presented to the LSRB.

(1) For laser systems and certification of laser firing ranges, contact the NSWCDD, Code G73, Dahlgren, VA, 22448, DSN 249-1060, commercial (540) 653-1060. Range surveys are also conducted by the Naval Surface Warfare Center, Corona Division, Code SE34, PO Box 5000, Corona, CA 92878, DSN 933-4143, commercial (909) 273-4143 or an administrative lead agent/LNTL-designated range laser safety specialist.

(2) For laser eyewear device evaluation, contact the Naval Air Warfare Center-Aircraft Division, NAWC-ACDIV Vision Laboratory, Code 4.6T, Patuxent River, MD, 20670, DSN 342-8480/8805, commercial (301) 342-8480/8805.

Enclosure (4)

MILITARY LASER EXEMPTION NOTIFICATION FORMAT

1. The following statement shall be used to notify the contractor that a laser product is exempt from 21 Code of Federal Regulations (CFR), chapter 1, subchapter J.

"In accordance with Exemption No. 76EL-01DoD to the Department of Defense on July 26, 1976, by the Commissioner of the Food and Drug Administration (FDA), the following electronic product is exempted from FDA radiation safety performance standards prescribed in 21 CFR, chapter 1, subchapter J.

Laser Type/Medium_____

Manufacturer_____

Number of Lasers/Systems_____

National Stock Number (if available_____

Local Stock Number_____

Reason for exemption:(check all that apply)

    Combat_____   Combat Training_____   Classified_____

2. The manufacturer shall label laser products exempted under 76EL-01DoD as follows:

CAUTION

This electronic product has been exempted from FDA radiation safety performance standards prescribed in the 21 CFR, chapter 1, subchapter J, under exemption No. 76EL-01 DoD issued on July 26, 1976. Use this product only with adequate protective devices or procedures.

or with other wording approved by the LSRB.

3. The contractor must comply with LSRB requirements and recommendations as stipulated in the contract, identify those design requirements of 21 CFR Part 1040 which cannot be incorporated in the system, and provide rationale for noncompliance with each requirement.

ACTIVITY LASER HAZARD CONTROL PROGRAM

1. <u>Introduction</u>. All activities that use military exempted, class 3B or class 4 lasers or systems incorporating any class 3B or class 4 lasers, or conduct maintenance on laser systems containing class 3B or class 4 lasers, shall establish a formal laser hazard control program. Medical facilities shall follow guidance as set forth by references (e), (f), (m), (n), and (o). A formal hazard control program is not required for class 1, 1M, 2, 2M, or 3R lasers and for optical fiber communication systems using lasers that comply with the design and operational procedures of American National Standards Institute Z136.2. (NOTE: Activities shall caution individuals using class 3a lasers labeled with a danger label and class 3R lasers that these devices are capable of causing severe eye damage).

2. <u>Program Requirements</u>. The activity laser hazard control program shall include as a minimum:

    a. <u>Regulations</u>. Establish an appropriate laser safety organization and issue laser safety regulations or standard operating procedures for indoor and outdoor operations and maintenance ensuring incorporation of hazard assessment and risk mitigation processes per reference (i).

    b. <u>Laser System Safety Officer (LSSO)</u>. The commanding officer shall designate an individual by name and code as the LSSO. Responsibilities and duties of the LSSO shall be formally documented to ensure that lasers are operated safely per this instruction. The LSSO shall have direct access to the commanding officer and have the authority to suspend, restrict, or terminate the operation of a laser or laser system. The LSSO shall be trained to perform his/her assigned duties. A detailed breakdown of Administrative Laser Safety Officer (ALSO), Technical Laser Safety Officer (TLSO), Laser Safety Specialist (LSS), and the Range Laser Safety Specialist (RLSS) qualifications are provided in enclosure (1). Retesting at the LSSO's highest level is required to maintain certification for all categories of LSSO every 4 years. Re-certification exams shall include prerequisite level information. If the LSSO fails the exam, the LSSO must be re-certified via the appropriate course.

    c. <u>Medical Laser Safety Officer</u>. Medical laser safety officers are a special case and must comply with reference (o) and do not have to be ALSO, TLSO, LSS, or RLSS certified, but must receive training that meets the requirements of reference (n). The commanding officer shall designate, in writing, an individual by name and code as the medical laser safety officer. Responsibilities and duties shall be formally documented to ensure that lasers are operated safely per this instruction. The medical laser safety officer shall have direct access to the commanding officer and have the authority to suspend, restrict, or terminate the operation of a laser or laser system. If the activity is a purely medical facility, then the designated medical laser safety officer can serve as the activity LSSO.

d. Laser Classification and Labeling. Each laser requires safety approval from the LSSO. Each laser also requires classification and labeling prior to use per enclosure (2). Some class 1 or class 2 lasers, when broken down for maintenance, allow class 3B or class 4 radiation levels to be accessible and are treated as class 3B or class 4 under those conditions. For example, if radiation at the level of class 3B or class 4 is accessible when a class 1 laser housing is removed, then procedures and labeling of the laser and maintenance manuals must warn of this condition. When a class 1 laser has a defeatable interlock that, when defeated, allows access to class 3B or class 4 emission levels, an additional label is needed on or near the access panel that states the following:

DANGER
Laser Radiation When Open and Interlock Defeated,
Avoid Eye or Skin Exposure to Direct or Scattered Radiation.

e. Protective Equipment. Commands using lasers shall provide appropriate laser protective equipment (e.g., eyewear (see enclosure 2), clothing, barriers, screens, etc.) to employees. Laser eye protection shall provide optical densities, at the operating wavelength(s), under both unaided and optically aided viewing (unless exempted by Laser Safety Review Board, to ensure that the applicable maximum permissible exposure is not exceeded. Eyewear shall be labeled with the wavelength and optical densities or appropriate laser eye protection code and inspected for serviceability prior to issue and at least annually to ensure its integrity. Any degradation such as cracks or bleaching shall result in replacement. Notify all concerned personnel of any defective eyewear.

f. Safety Evaluations, Inspections and Surveys. Laser facilities and ranges (other than medical facilities) shall receive local laser safety compliance inspections annually by a TLSO, LSS, or RLSS. Medical facilities shall be inspected on setup and per references (e), (f), (n), and (o). Naval Surface Warfare Center (NSWC), Dahlgren Division, NSWC Corona Division, or an Administrative Lead Agent (ALA)/Lead Navy Technical Laboratory (LNTL)-certified RLSS shall perform complete laser radiation hazard surveys and evaluations on laser ranges to determine the degree of laser radiation hazard and to recommend proper controls. These hazard surveys and evaluations shall be performed on all new laser ranges and on portions of a certified range that want to incorporate changes. These ranges must be re-certified every 3 years.

g. <u>Medical Surveillance Program</u>. A laser medical surveillance program shall be established and maintained per reference (m).

h. <u>Laser Inventory</u>. Maintain and submit all necessary records required by reference (c) and other government regulations to the ALA and Technical Lead Agent (TLA). Maintain a list of all class 3B, class 4 and military exempt lasers and their locations at the activity. A current laser inventory and all records for lost or disposed laser systems shall be maintained for submission to the ALA and TLA per paragraph 7e(7) of this instruction. Inventory sheets are included in enclosures (10) and (11) of this instruction.

i. <u>Warning Devices and Signs</u>. Post laser warning devices and signs at appropriate locations to protect unsuspecting personnel from laser radiation per reference (b) and enclosures (2) and (6) through (9).

j. <u>Documented Safety Duties for Laser Supervisors</u>. Document the safety responsibilities of personnel who supervise laser operations. During laser operations a trained laser supervisor is required. Those duties may include such functions as safety planning for the installation of laser systems, providing and enforcing operational procedures, ensuring employees receive appropriate training, investigating incidents, and logging class 3B and class 4 laser firings.

k. <u>Operator Training and Certification</u>. Conduct a command laser safety training program per enclosure (7). Prior to assignment, employees who work with lasers shall receive formal training in methods of hazard control. Establish procedures to qualify a laser operator or maintenance technician worker.

Procedures shall include periodic review to ensure that personnel are complying with requirements such as annual refresher training. Per reference (d), construction workers shall have proof of their training readily available or in their possession.

l. <u>Emergency Provisions</u>. The emergency procedures (to include emergency shutdown procedures, laser hazard information, and points of contact) shall be posted at each laser installation in a location that is safely accessible to personnel rendering emergency aid. Emergency medical technicians and firefighters shall be trained in laser hazards and controls. This may require liaison with outside (contractor) personnel.

m. <u>Laser Safety Committee</u>. Establish a local laser safety committee to assist in discharging the above responsibilities if warranted by the magnitude of the potential hazards in local operations.

n. <u>Laser Mishap Investigation</u>. Ensure prompt medical attention is given to laser injuries. Investigate and report laser mishaps per references (e), (f), (g), and (m). Copies of reports shall be sent to the Naval Safety Center, Bureau of Medicine and Surgery (M3B4), Headquarters Marine Corps Safety Division, the LNTL and the ALA per references (e), (f), and (g). Ensure corrective actions are taken to prevent similar mishaps.

o. <u>Disposal of Military Exempt Lasers</u>. Obtain ALA approval prior to disposal of military exempt lasers. Ensure excess military exempt lasers are not sold or donated outside the Department of the Defense unless they have been brought into compliance with 21 Code of Federal Regulations and received Food and Drug Administration registration and ALA approval. Disposition/disposal shall be in accordance with reference (k), with demilitarization in accordance with reference (l).

GENERAL REQUIREMENTS FOR LASER HAZARD CONTROL

1. <u>General</u>

    a. All military exempt and class 3B and class 4 lasers, used in airborne, at sea or military ground operations shall be reviewed and approved by the Navy Laser Safety Review Board (LSRB) prior to their use to determine compliance with regulations, laser hazard data, and recommended eye protection.

    b. Only properly trained and authorized personnel shall operate Class 3B and 4 laser devices.

    c. Every laser operation or series of laser firings using class 3B or class 4 laser systems shall be logged for all outdoor range operations by the hosting range and operational unit, and for all laboratory firings/tests by laboratory personnel. Documentation for training and combat operations shall include the start and stop time of the exercise/operation regardless of the number of firings; documenting each on/off cycle of the laser is preferred and should be done whenever practical. Documentation for lasers used in a laboratory shall include each on/off cycle of the laser. An example log is provided in figure 7-1. Logs shall be maintained per reference (q) SSIC 8140.2.

    d. Personnel shall not be allowed access to a controlled lasing area (for example, laboratory, laser range, or laser-firing area) unless they have had a hazard brief, the appropriate supervisory approval has been obtained, and protective measures have been taken.

    e. Prior to laser operations, the operator shall ensure that the laser target area, laser hazard zone and/or laboratory is clear of personnel or that any personnel within the area are aware of imminent laser operation and are properly protected against laser hazards.

    f. Unprotected personnel shall not be exposed to laser radiation in excess of the Maximum Permissible Exposure (MPE) levels in reference (b).

        (1) Personnel shall use personal protective equipment specifically designed for protection against the laser system when engineering or procedural controls are inadequate to eliminate radiation levels in excess of the MPE.

(2) Laser protective eyewear shall be marked with optical density values and wavelength for which protection is afforded or the appropriate laser eye protection code and issued to involved personnel. The eyewear shall provide a snug fit and shall not be used if it does not pass inspection. Before each use and during periodic (at least annual) Laser System Safety Officer (LSSO) safety inspections, laser eye protection shall be inspected for:

(a) Pitting, crazing, scratching, cracking, bleaching, etc.

(b) Mechanical integrity and leaks.

(3) Optical systems such as lenses, telescopes, etc., may increase the hazard to the eye and may be used only when appropriate interlocks or filters are used to attenuate the radiation levels below the MPE. Contact lead Navy technical laboratory or a certified laser safety specialist for assistance in calculations and evaluation of optical systems and filters.

g. All laser systems used in combat, combat training, or used on ranges shall have boresight verification per LSRB requirements.

2. Warning signs. Laser range and building warning signs as shown in figures 7-2 and 7-3 of this enclosure shall be posted at the entrances to laser ranges, buildings, or rooms.

3. Non-beam hazards

a. Commands shall make provision to protect against hazardous by-products that may result from the reaction of laser radiation, especially ultraviolet laser radiation, with air, plastics, and other substances such as ozone and skin irritants.

b. Personnel shall not be exposed to microwave power densities in excess of those specified in reference (e).

c. Appropriate precautions shall be taken per environmental, safety and health policy and guidance for the non-beam hazards in laser installations that may arise from the following:

(1) Electricity;

(2) Cryogenics;

(3) Compressed gas;

(4) Toxic materials;

(5) Noise;

(6) Arc of filament lamps;

(7) Targets that may shatter;

(8) Ionizing radiation;

(9) Incoherent optical and ultraviolet radiation from laser discharge tubes, flash lamps or laser/target plasmas;

(10) Charged capacitors; and

(11) Flash lamp or capacitor explosion.

d. Proper personnel protection and procedures shall be provided in the use of cryogenics. Compressed gas bottles shall be secured. All laser discharge tubes or flash lamps, the laser target, capacitors, and all elements of the optical train that may shatter shall be contained. All incidental radiation shall be adequately shielded. Toxic materials shall be so marked and adequately controlled. Smoking, eating, or drinking in laser work areas shall be prohibited.

4. Training for Operators/Maintainers

a. All personnel in areas using class 3B or class 4 lasers and all personnel using class 3a or class 3R force-on-force lasers shall receive annual training about the potential hazard associated with accidental exposure to this form of radiation. In particular, the extraordinary danger of eye damage due to focusing and absorption by the eyes shall be emphasized. Class 3B and class 4 lasers may also cause skin damage or damage to material by fire or explosion due to rapid heating from a focused beam. Initial safety training and refresher training shall be appropriate to the operation. Topics for training shall include but not be limited to:

(1) Laser fundamentals including associated beam and non-beam hazards. Include a discussion of the hazards associated with class 3a laser devices with danger labels or class 3R lasers.

(2) Standard operating procedures, laser system specifications, hazard data, and control measures for laser systems appropriate to the individual's job to minimize risk of accidental exposure to personnel.

(3) Manufacturer's operating information, LSRB safety information and any other safety requirements (to include non-beam hazards) or procedures specific to the command-used system(s).

(4) Type of eye protection to be worn and any other personal protective equipment required.

(5) Review of medical surveillance program/requirements (reference (m)).

(6) Review of local range standard operating procedures/ regulations (for operators and laser range personnel).

(7) Review of maintenance precautions/requirements (for personnel conducting maintenance on laser devices that potentially exposes them or other personnel to the beam).

b. Other topics should be at the discretion of the supervisor in conjunction with the LSSO and may consist of information interchange seminars between laser users on the usefulness of existing safety procedures, information on recently discovered hazards/hazardous materials or suggestions for new safety devices.

5. <u>Laser, Associated Support Equipment, and Facilities Design Safety Features</u>

a. Each laser, regardless of class, must have protective housings to prevent excessive optical and X-radiation. All laser protective housings must be interlocked. When the protective housing containing the laser beam is not interlocked or has defeatable interlocks, a warning sign must be provided stating "CAUTION" or "DANGER" (depending on the internal laser classification) with additional information concerning the hazard involved.

b. Other laser safety requirements include an emission indicator that provides a visible signal when viewed through protective goggles, or an audible warning signal during laser radiation emission in excess of the maximum allowable safe limits. The warning signal must not cause personnel to inadvertently look into the laser beam or reflected radiation from the target. Personnel should be made aware of the meaning of this emission indicator. Each class 3B or class 4 laser must be supplied with a beam attenuator capable of preventing unsafe levels of laser radiation. This attenuator shall be used whenever possible especially during maintenance. Class 3B and class 4 laser area access should be interlocked with the laser system to prevent accidental radiation of personnel. Where this is not feasible, a Nominal Hazard Zone (NHZ) may be defined and enforced instead of interlocking entrances to general laser work areas. The use of electric eyes and warning alarms is recommended to assist in policing the perimeter of the NHZ.

c. All non-exempted lasers to be used by the military or on a military installation must be designed and built per reference (a). Associated support equipment, facilities, protective eyewear, and operating and maintenance procedures shall be per reference (b), manufacturer instructions, and LSRB requirements, where applicable. All optical fiber communication systems shall include the requirements of reference (p). All military exempt lasers, their associated support equipment, facilities, and eye protection shall be designed and constructed per enclosure (2).

6. Construction Lasers. In addition to the general rules, follow Occupational Safety and Health Administration regulations of reference (d) for lasers used in construction.

LASER FIRING LOG

Command

_____

Range

_____

Date

_____

System

_____

User

_____

Mission Commander

_____

Firing # Time	Target Location	Firing Position/Heading
_____	_____	_____
_____	_____	_____
_____	_____	_____
_____	_____	_____
_____	_____	_____
_____	_____	_____
_____	_____	_____
_____	_____	_____
_____	_____	_____

Figure 7-1. Sample Laser Firing Log

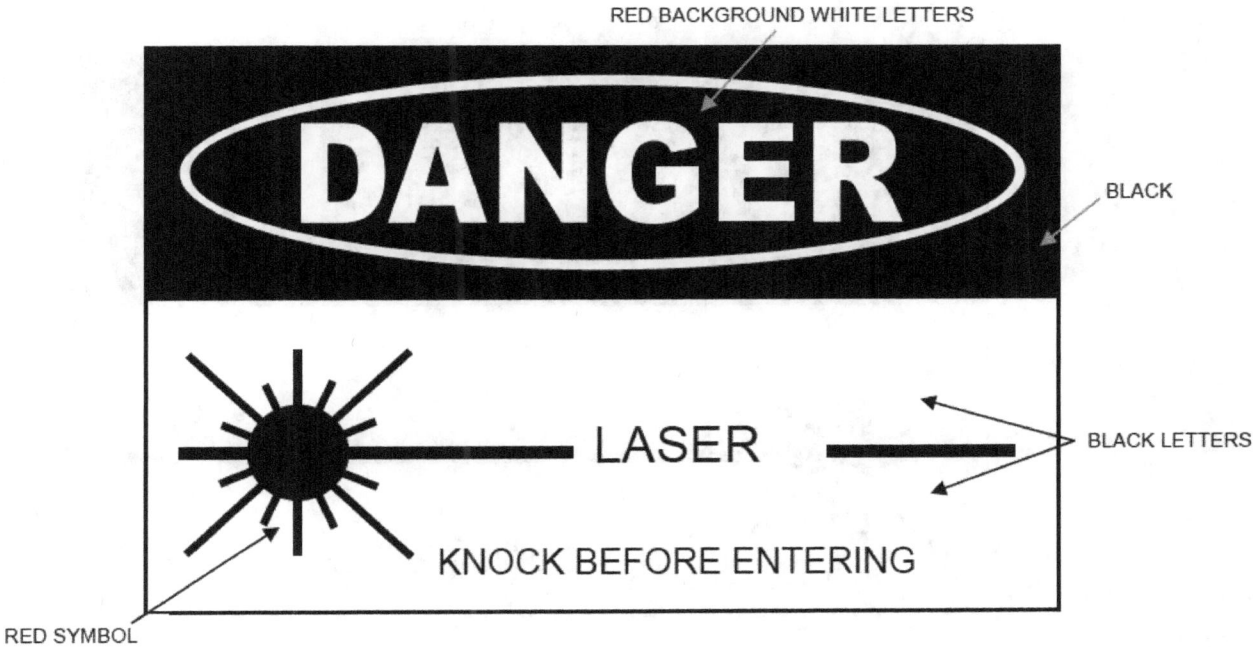

Laser Maintenance Area Warning Sign

[Source: ANSI Z136.1, Safe Use of Lasers]

Figure 7-2. Example of a Laser Maintenance Area Warning Sign

Laser Range Warning Sign

Available at: https://navalforms.daps.dla.mil
Stock Number: 0118LF0201100
Form Number: NAVSEA 1995/17

Figure 7-3. Example of a Laser Range Warning Sign

SAFETY REQUIREMENTS FOR MILITARY LASER RANGES

1. <u>Introduction</u>. All laser device/system control requirements of enclosures (6) and (7) apply in addition to the following range-specific information.

2. <u>General</u>

     a. Range safety personnel with laser safety training and experience appropriate to the exercise or operation shall be present during all laser operations.

     b. When ground positions are designating for aircraft, an aircraft exclusion zone shall be established that is centered on the ground-lasing position to the target. The exclusion zone shall be, at a minimum, a 20-degree safety cone around the firing point extending back from the target to the firing point.

     c. During airborne laser operations, personnel in the lasing aircraft must wear laser protective eyewear in single aircraft laser scenarios if there is a possibility of retro-reflectors or other flat specular reflectors in the target area and within one-half the nominal ocular hazard distances from the aircraft.

     d. All personnel in other aircraft that must fly in the restricted airspace through a defined laser hazard area must have suitable laser protective eyewear in place during transit of that hazard area. Note that if more than one aircraft is or may be lasing during the operation, all personnel in all aircraft shall wear suitable laser protective eyewear while in the hazard zone.

     e. Class 3B and class 4 laser target designators and rangefinders shall not be activated until a designated target has been acquired optically or through a recognized tracking system (e.g., forward looking infrared or radar). Laser target locators and illuminators require special care during use to avoid illuminating non-target areas.

     f. No class 3B or class 4 lasers shall be directed above the horizon unless coordinated with the Federal Aviation Administration and affected Department of Defense components, including North American Aerospace Defense Command, CMOC/J3, Attn: Orbital Safety Officer, Cheyenne Mountain AFS, CO 80914-6020, Laser Clearinghouse, DSN 268-4416, (719) 474-4416.

g. All ship-towed targets shall adhere to requirements of reference (j).

3. <u>Range Certification</u>. Naval Surface Warfare Center (NSWC), Dahlgren Division, NSWC Corona Division, or an Administrative Lead Agent/Lead Navy Technical Laboratory-certified Range Laser Safety Specialist(RLSS) shall perform complete laser radiation hazard surveys and evaluations of laser ranges to determine the degree of laser radiation hazard and to recommend proper controls. These hazard surveys and evaluations shall be performed on all new laser ranges, whenever changes to the range invalidates the current certification and every 3 years. Copies of all range certifications shall be forwarded to NSWC Corona. Additionally, laser facilities and laser ranges shall receive local safety compliance inspections annually by a technical laser safety officer, laser safety specialist or RLSS.

4. <u>Range Regulations/Range Standard Operating Procedures (SOP)</u>. Every laser range complex shall develop and maintain a range SOP. The SOP should contain, at a minimum, a description of the authorized firing points, run-in headings, altitude restrictions, firing fans, and other control measures and restrictions for the range.

5. <u>Laser System Safety Officer/Command Responsibilities</u>

a. The Range Laser Safety Officer (RLSO) for the hosting range complex shall:

(1) Ensure requesting unit has a certified Laser System Safety Officer (LSSO) coordinating the test/training operation. The LSSO need not be on scene if a trained laser supervisor is present.

(2) Provide the local range regulations/standard operating procedures to the LSSO of the requesting unit.

(3) Review proposed laser range operations plan or test plan to ensure compliance with current certification and local regulations and standard operating procedures.

(4) Ensure a laser safety inspection of the range is completed prior to its use (e.g., signs are posted, area is clear of specular reflectors, laser eye protection is available, etc.).

(5) Ensure only tactics authorized within the scope of the range certification and only Laser Safety Review Board-approved laser systems are used for the operation/exercise/test.

b. The command requesting use of the laser range shall:

(1) Review host range complex range regulations/SOP.

(2) Provide a range use operations plan/test plan to RLSO that includes:

(a) Name and date of qualification of the command LSSO;

(b) Laser devices to be used;

(c) Laser device firing points, firing areas, or firing lines;

(d) Targets to be used/target areas to be used;

(e) Ground personnel locations (indicating those requiring laser eye protection);

(f) Laser eye protection to be used (if applicable);

(g) Aircraft run-in headings (if applicable);

(h) Ship heading for towed target operations (if applicable);

(i) Laser mode(s)/tactics to be employed (e.g., force-on-force, designation, rangefinding, offset lasing, high altitude release bomb, etc.);

(j) Hazard areas to be cleared of non-operating personnel (roadblock locations, if required);

(k) Types of surveillance to be used to ensure a clear range; and

(l) Radio frequencies (or channels) and standardized terminology for communication where appropriate.

(3) Ensure all personnel involved in operations receive an appropriate pre-mission brief to include:

(a) Authorized tactics, firing positions, firing fans, and aircraft run-in headings (as appropriate);

(b) Drawings, photographs, descriptions or grid points of authorized targets;

(c) Communication procedures that include specific frequencies (or channels), controlling authorities, and standardized terminology;

(d) Acquisition, identification, and tracking procedures for targets are established prior to laser activation;

(e) Missile/ordnance mode of operation (as appropriate for live fire operations);

(f) Requirements for beam termination;

(g) Control measures to minimize the risk of unauthorized personnel or aircraft entering the range area;

(h) Type of eye protection to be worn (if applicable);

(i) Potential hazards posed by the laser system (e.g., phantom targeting and backscatter); the target area, maintenance area, etc.; types of warning signs to be posted; and specific procedures to avoid these hazards (as appropriate); and

(j) Conduct and brief the hazard assessment plan per OPNAVINST 3500.39B (reference (i)).

(4) Ensure appropriate laser eye protection is provided and worn by all personnel within the laser hazard zone.

(5) Ensure all aspects of the range regulations/standard operating procedures are adhered to during the operation/exercise/test.

LABORATORY LASER USE AND LASER MAINTENANCE REQUIREMENTS

1. <u>General</u>. Use of all class 3B and class 4 lasers in laboratory settings and all lasers requiring maintenance that could expose personnel to laser radiation exceeding the Maximum Permissible Exposure (MPE) shall adhere to the requirements in reference (o) and enclosures (6) and (7). Additionally, the requirements of this enclosure apply:

2. <u>Laboratory Use of Lasers</u>.

   a. At least two people should be present at all times when operating lasers with accessible high voltage. Where the operation allows, follow a countdown procedure to minimize unnecessary potential exposure by forewarning personnel to take necessary protection from the radiation by donning protective equipment or moving out of the danger area. Operators shall verify that conditions are safe before proceeding.

   b. Lasers and laser beams should be contained within suitably controlled equipment, spaces, or ranges. Laser beams emitted by an unenclosed system must be terminated at the end of the useful beam path if the exposure level is greater than the MPE. The backstop shall be of material that absorbs or blocks the particular wavelength and shall not burn or emit toxic products when irradiated. Special care in absorbing and containing the laser radiation must be taken especially when the laser is emitting energy in the ultraviolet or infrared portions of the spectrum where the observer might receive damage to the eyes without being aware of the direct radiation or its reflection. Laser controls must be located to prevent operator exposure to unsafe levels of radiation. Care should be taken to block all extraneous radiation such as that reflected or refracted from materials used to interact with laser beams.

   c. Reflecting surfaces that are not specifically approved for use in the exercise, such as mirrors, bottles, windows, shiny metal, plexiglas, or other surfaces that have a high coefficient of specular reflection shall be eliminated from the beam path or shall be faced and surrounded with diffuse absorbing substances to absorb the energy prior to operations. Personnel working in the vicinity of laser beams shall not wear jewelry such as watches or tie clasps that could act as specular reflectors.

d. Laboratory laser operating procedures shall be posted outside each entrance to the area where lasers are operated or maintained. The standard operating procedure shall address, where feasible, each laser used therein by name and shall include:

    (1) Lasers authorized;

    (2) Normal operations;

    (3) Entry restrictions;

    (4) Types of protective eyewear required (wavelength and optical density);

    (5) Startup safety requirements (types and locations of beam stops, countdown procedures, area clearance procedures, warning lights activated outside and inside the area, etc.);

    (6) Emergency shutdown procedures for fire, rescue, and security personnel in case of emergency. (NOTE: This information should be on file with fire, rescue, and security personnel as well.);

    (7) Conditions for unattended operation if permitted by the Laser System Safety Officer (LSSO);

    (8) Exact hazardous material allowed and conditions of permitted use, including personal protective equipment, fire fighting equipment, ventilation requirements, storage containers, allowed amounts, and emergency response procedures;

    (9) Specific prohibitions (e.g., no smoking or flames, no eating or drinking); and

    (10) Requirement for two persons to be present during operations for emergency assistance where deemed necessary by the LSSO.

3. Laser Maintenance. Some lasers classified as class 1, 2, 3a, or 3R may contain an embedded class 3B or class 4 laser that changes the class when attenuator, panels, or protective housings are removed for servicing and maintenance.

a. General

(1) During maintenance, hazardous levels of laser radiation shall be confined to prevent exposure of unprotected personnel. Such confinement may consist of:

(a) An enclosure which safely confines the radiation with no specular (mirror-like) reflections, and is adequately interlocked or guarded and provided with exterior warning lights (as appropriate) and warning signs similar to figure 7-2;

(b) An output lens cap that safely confines the radiation; and

(c) When removal of panels, attenuator, or protective housings; overriding of protective housing interlocks; or entry into the nominal hazard zone leads to accessible laser radiation exceeding the MPE, a temporary laser controlled area with the signs and precautions appropriate to the class 3B or class 4 laser shall be devised. Additionally, a cap shall be provided to cover the laser radiation exit port to prevent undesired or unauthorized external radiation.

(2) Maintenance protocols shall be posted in and around the controlled area where personnel could be exposed to laser radiation in excess of the MPE. Maintenance protocols shall include:

(a) Laser device and its hazard parameters;

(b) Authorized protective eye wear; and

(c) Procedures in the event of laser over exposure (to include points of contacts with verified phone numbers and procedures to shut down the laser).

(3) All safety devices including cutouts and eyewear shall be checked and maintained on a regular basis.

(4) All electrical safety precautions of references (e) and (f), the Interactive Electronic Technician Manual for Navy Installation and Maintenance Books, N0002400003, Occupational Safety and Health Administration standards 29 Code of Federal Regulations Parts 1910, 1915, and 1926 shall be strictly enforced, especially in the use of grounding rods to discharge

capacitors and the two-person rule (where two persons are cardiopulmonary resuscitation trained).

(5) Precautions and protection shall be provided against noise in excess of 84 decibels(A), radiation, hazardous material such as some lens coatings and connector compounds, toxic or inert gases, cryogenics, mechanical hazards, radiation through viewing ports, and other recognized hazards.

b. <u>Optical Fiber Communication Systems (OFCS)</u>. OFCS that contain lasers shall be considered enclosed systems as long as the laser remains fully attached to the cable and the radiation output is confined within a cable system. Any laser fiber optic connector that is not inside a secured equipment enclosure shall be labeled with the caution or danger appropriate to the laser and shall require a tool to be disconnected. While no tool for disconnection is required when the connector is located inside a secured equipment enclosure, caution or danger signs appropriate to the class of the laser shall be located near the connectors and shall be visible when the enclosure is open. The local LSSO shall ensure that the following general rules are applied when servicing OFCSs:

(1) Detachable components and connectors are labeled;

(2) Continuity with an optical test set has been verified; and

(3) Employees' laser hazard training includes the potential hazards associated with looking into broken or disconnected cables.

EXAMPLE OF MILITARY EXEMPT LASER INVENTORY FORMAT

From:

To: Chief, Bureau of Medicine and Surgery (M3B4)

Subj: EXEMPT LASER INVENTORY REPORT FOR FY

INSTRUCTIONS: Lasers should be grouped. All lasers included on
one entry sheet must have identical characteristics, i.e., same
contract number, same National Stock Number (NSN), same
function, same delivery date, same disposal date, etc. Only
their serial numbers and plant account numbers can be different.
List beginning and ending serial/plant account numbers for
continuous sequences. If classified, any field except contract
number may be left blank for reasons of national security.

System Name_____ AN/_____

Type_____ Class_____
Manufacturer_____

Approved by LSRB? (Y)___   (N)___   If no,
explain_____

Exemption Qualification (Check applicable spaces)
     Combat_____ Training_____ Classified_____

Optional: Contract Number_____

          Total to date in this contract_____

          NSN_____ Serial
     Numbers_____

STATUS

Subtotals should add up to quantity possessed. Disposed lasers shall be
maintained as a separate part of the inventory. Lost lasers shall be
reported immediately to the administrative lead agent (ALA).

Quantity Possessed _____

Subtotals: In use_____ Repair_____ Storage_____ Await Disposal_____

Laser Location(s) _____

Custodian Name(s)_____

Phone_____   Signature(s)_____

                                 _____

EXAMPLE OF NON-MILITARY EXEMPT CLASS 3B AND CLASS 4 LASER INVENTORY FORMAT

From:

To: Chief, Bureau of Medicine and Surgery (M3B4)

Subj: CLASS 3B AND CLASS 4 LASER INVENTORY REPORT FOR FY

Laser Name_____

Type_____

Wavelength_____   Max. Output_____

Pulse or continuous wave (CW) _____   Class_____

Program/User/Custodian
Name(s)_____

Phone_____

Location(s)_____

Use(s)_____

Optional: Manufacturer_____

          Contract Number_____

          NSN_____

          Plant Account Numbers_____

          Serial Number(s)_____

                          Signature(s)_____

                          _____

                          _____

                          _____

LASER SAFETY REQUIREMENTS SUMMARY

X – shall
O – should
blank – not required

LASER SAFETY REQUIREMENTS SUMMARY	All lasers used in combat, combat training and classified in the interest of national security					Other lasers						
						All Locations			Indoor Lab/Test		Range	
	1/1M	2/2M	3a/3R	3B	4	1/1M	2/2M	3a/3R¹	3B	4	3B	4
OPNAVINST 5100.23G (ashore)²/OPNAVINST 5100.19E² (afloat)/This instruction	X	X	X	X	X	X	X	X	X	X	X	X
SECNAVINST 5100.14D	X	X	X	X	X							
LSRB APPROVAL	X	X	X	X	X	O	O	O	O	O	X	X
21 CFR (FDA REGISTERED)	X	X	X	X	X	X	X	X	X	X	X	X
LASER SAFETY DESIGN REQUIREMENT CHECKLIST ADAPTED FROM MIL-STD-1425A			X	X	X							
MAINTAIN INVENTORY	X	X	X	X	X				X	X	X	X
APPROVAL FOR DISPOSAL FROM ADMINISTRATIVE LEAD AGENT (ALA)	X	X	X	X	X							
T&E BY LNTL	X	X	X	X	X	O	O	O	O	O	X	X
CONTRACTING OFFICER NOTIFY CONTRACTOR CONCERNING EXEMPTION AND LABELING PER ENCL (3)	X	X	X	X	X							
CAUTION LABEL PER ANSI Z136.1		X	X									
DANGER LABEL PER ANSI Z136.1				X	X							
CAUTION LABEL PER 21 CFR							X	X				
DANGER LABEL PER 21 CFR									X	X	X	X
USER TRAINING Read manufacturer literature and labeling	X	X	X	X	X	X	X	X				
Formal safety specific training with demo/military video			X	X	X			X	X	X	X	X
LASER SYSTEM SAFETY OFFICER ASSIGNED & TRAINED	X	X	X	X	X				X	X	X	X
LASER INST PROMULGATED	X	X	X	X	X				X	X	X	X
MIL-HDBK-828A	X	X	X	X	X				X	X	X	X

1 For lasers that exceed class 3a or class 3R limits for aided viewing additional requirements may apply

2 Required for Navy commands

RESTRICTIONS

Class 1 Lasers	Class 2 Lasers	Class 3a Lasers with CAUTION LABEL and Class 1M and 2M Lasers[1]	Class 3a Lasers with DANGER LABEL and Class 3R Lasers
None during operation.	Caution label and prohibition against staring into beam.	Caution label on laser and prohibition against staring into beam or viewing with optical aids.	Danger label on laser and prohibition against looking into beam or viewing with optical aids.

[1]Note: Class 1M and class 2M laser when viewed with magnifying optics may reach class 3B or class 4 hazard levels.

RESTRICTIONS AT LABORATORIES AND TEST FACILITIES

Class 3B Lasers	Class 4 Lasers
Danger sign and warning light or other indicator on laser and lab entrance.	Same as Class 3B.
Elimination of all unnecessary specular reflectors from beam path and insertion of beam stops around all remaining specular reflectors.	Removal of hazardous diffuse reflectors.
Beam stops or enclosed beam path.	Nonflammable stops where necessary.
Safety procedures for operations and maintenance posted or on hand.	Skin protection when necessary.
Flat paint on surfaces (walls, etc.).	Special precautions for high energy.
Adequate illumination appropriate to the task.	
Protective eyewear at the specific wavelength and proper optical density (OD). (Unnecessary and unsafe use of protective eyewear shall be avoided.)	
Protective eyewear training, inspection, and replacement program in place.	

Class 3B Lasers	Class 4 Lasers
Entrance interlocks if beam is not enclosed (interlocks may insert beam stop over exit port of laser or disconnect power to laser.) or if other electrical/chemical/physical hazards exist to entrants. Other techniques such as door locks (doors should open for emergency egress and during power loss.), entry alarms, entrance sentries, beam controls, etc., when approved by the Laser System Safety Officer (LSSO).	
Emergency shutdown switch per enclosure (2).	
Key lock master switch.	
See section 7 of American National Standard Institute Z136.1, paragraph 5 and enclosure (2) for more details.	

RESTRICTIONS AT RANGES[1]

Class 3B Lasers	Class 4 Lasers
Laser safety survey and certification by trained and qualified range laser safety specialist, the lead Navy technical laboratory, or Naval Surface Warfare Center Corona	Same as Class 3B and:
Survey and recertification required every 3 years or after each range modification.	Elimination of hazardous diffuse reflectors
Danger warning signs posted per this instruction at range boundaries and entrances and at the laser.	Nonflammable absorbing beam stops where necessary.
Barricades with DANGER/WARNING signs on access roads to target area.	Skin protection where necessary.

Class 3B Lasers	Class 4 Lasers
Target area, buffer zone, and nonreflecting beam stop assigned for each specific laser.	Special precautions for high energy sources.
Target area and targets free of specular reflectors.	
Protective eyewear at the specific wavelengths and proper OD on personnel in restricted areas (target area and buffer zone).[2]	
Protective eyewear training, inspection, and replacement program in place.	
Range log of time, date, and heading of laser firing.	
Adequate area surveillance.	
Two-way communications between range safety officer, laser personnel, and restricted area personnel.	
Target in cross hairs on laser sight before lasing.	
Lasing ceased when directed by range control or if unable to keep target in sights.	
A clearing pass by aircraft before lasing or other suitable means, as determined by the range laser system safety officer, of insuring range is clear.	
Restricted airspace and time established where laser radiation is potentially in flight path of aircraft or satellites.	
Safe flight profile of allowed laser operating altitudes, headings, and distances from target maintained by lasing aircraft.	
Area of restriction established for other aircraft within the nominal hazard distance of the laser.	
Personnel in other aircraft in the restricted cone around the laser line of sight having eye protection of proper OD and wavelength.	

Class 3B Lasers	Class 4 Lasers
For ground laser operations, assurance that all unprotected personnel are behind the laser and are not within the buffer zone anywhere along the laser line of sight, or between the laser and target or between target and backstop.	
Presence of range safety personnel with appropriate laser safety training and experience during all laser operations.	
All range personnel involved with laser operations trained in laser safety.	
A medical surveillance program in place per BUMEDINST 6470.23 series.	
Only lasers approved by the Navy LSRB in use.	
Range adequately controlled to prevent unauthorized entry.	

[1] Comply with MIL-HDBK-828A.
[2] Enclosure 6, provides background